30 Second Timeout

Kevin Wolma

Copyright © 2020 Kevin Wolma
All rights reserved.
979-8-635-78251-4

INTRODUCTION

One of the most challenging aspects of being a parent is navigating our way through the world of youth sports. In what activities do I involve my kids and at what age? When do I put them on a travel sports team? For which travel organization do we have our children play? How much money are we willing to spend? What if we do all of this and they still do not make the high school team?

This book took ten years to write because each of these chapters is either an experience I have dealt with as a parent for the last eighteen years or a challenge I have witnessed in my role as a high school coach and athletic director over the past twenty-five.

Why the title *30 Second Timeout*? I am a former basketball coach, and when things would begin to unravel on the court, I would call a "30 second timeout" to regain the team's focus. Regardless if you are a parent of a child in little league, AYSO soccer, or varsity athletics, you will experience instances when you'll need to take a "30 second timeout" to regain your own focus.

Whether we're tempted to yell at the officials for a missed call or at our own children for making a mistake, all of us, occasionally, need to take a "30 second timeout." Maybe we need to take a "30 second timeout" as we worry about our child earning an athletic scholarship or even as we celebrate his or her athletic accomplishments. In any case, I hope that this book will provide insight and awareness to help parents and their athletes deal with all of these issues and much more.

The purpose of this book is to communicate, explore, and advise on all of today's challenges accompanying our children's participation in athletics. My hope is that *30 Second Timeout* is a valuable resource which will enhance not only your experience in educational athletics, but that of your children as well.

This is an incredible odyssey, along which we will explore every possible emotion. We will sometimes be moved to cheer and we will sometimes encounter disappointment. We will, at times, feel anger and at other times, pride. Together, they all give each of us an opportunity to grow in areas we never thought possible. Please join me on this crazy but extremely rewarding journey we can all negotiate together

CONTENTS

	ACKNOWLEDGEMENTS	i
1	YOUTH SPORTS PARENT ATHLETIC CREED	1
2	WHAT REALLY DRIVES RESULTS	3
3	CAN WE TEACH SPORTSMANSHIP?	7
4	WHEN TIME STANDS STILL	11
5	THE PARENT COACH	15
6	PLEASE OPEN THE DOOR!	19
7	COACHING FROM THE STANDS	23
8	CHASING AFTER THE WIND	25
9	WHAT DO YOU STAND FOR?	29
10	WHAT CAN YOU LEARN FROM A 4TH GRADE TEACHER?	33
11	CUTS	37
12	WHAT HAPPENS WHEN THE GAME IS OVER?	41
13	WHY SO LOUD?	45
14	DEALING WITH THE UNEXPECTED	49
15	ADVERSITY	53
16	WHAT DID YOU SAY?	55
17	THE GAME OUTSIDE OF THE GAME	59
18	ARE YOU INVOLVED OR COMMITTED?	63
19	ONE WORD	67
20	PARTNERSHIP	71
21	MOTIVATION	75
22	PERSPECTIVE	79
23	OFFICIALS	81
24	RELEASE	85
25	CHOICES	89
26	BIG MIKE CHALLENGE	93
27	WHAT IS YOUR IMAGE?	97
28	YOU SEE WHAT YOU WANT TO SEE	101
29	IMPACT OF BODY LANGUAGE ON SPORTS	105
30	IT'S OVER	109

ACKNOWLEDGMENTS

I have so many people to thank. My wife Gina has been the rock in our family. While my career has required that I spend the majority of my time watching thousands of other kids play sports, Gina has been the one managing our three kids' schedules while making sure she is present at all of their events. I have learned more about being a parent from her than anyone else. Gina, I love you!

My kids Jordan, Kayla, and Kelsey are amazing! They have brought more joy to my life than I could have ever imagined, and their passion for living is an inspiration to me. It has been an incredible journey watching them grow and I can't wait to see where their next chapters of life take them. I love each of you!

A special thank you to Paul Zielinski who has poured hours into reading this manuscript while always providing great feedback and suggestions. There is no way I could have done this without you.

At Hudsonville we have some very talented students. I want to say a special thank you to one of those students, Steven St. John, for his creativity with the design of this book cover.

I truly have been blessed to live and work in Hudsonville, Michigan. Hudsonville Public Schools took a chance on me as an educator, then as a coach, and now as the district's Athletic Director. So many fellow teachers, coaches, and administrators have had an impact on me that it would take another book to name them all. What an absolute honor it has been both to serve our student-athletes every day and to be blessed with the opportunity to work beside an incredible staff of coaches who truly care about transformational athletics. Thank you!

Finally, a special thanks to Jon Gordon. Just over ten years ago I read a book called *The Energy Bus* that changed my life forever. The significance of a positive attitude has spilled over into how I try to live my life as a teacher, coach, administrator, and parent. His books have inspired me to write my own. I hope that this provides some positivity and perspective to readers' lives.

YOUTH SPORTS PARENT ATHLETIC CREED

Every one of us wants athletics to be a tremendous, holistic experience for our kids, but to what extreme will parents go to attain success for their own children? Many parents place high demands on coaches not only to win games, but to showcase their child while doing it. They are also critical of officials, hoping to ensure their own best possible outcome. What I hope parents realize is that through their actions and words in the stands, on the car ride home, and at the dinner table, they can play an incredible role when it comes to creating a culture of excellence.

This "Youth Sports Parent Athletic Creed" will allow each parent, coach, and official the opportunity to make this a truly rewarding experience for our kids. This creed will also provide each of our student-athletes an opportunity to grow not only physically, but mentally and emotionally as well. Finally, it is meant to offer parents a roadmap to success so they can likewise enjoy the experience.

Youth Sports Parent Athletic Creed

1. **Parents will understand their role.** Parents will parent, players will play, coaches will coach, and officials will officiate. If you want your athlete to play at his/her highest level, make sure the coach is listened to and respected. Mixed messages from you will only cause confusion and a decrease in your child's performance level.

2. **Parents will equally support and encourage their child and his/her teammates and coaches, no matter the outcome.** If you want to build a solid relationship with your child, then after every game--win or lose--express that you love to watch him/her play along with a reminder to keep listening to the coach.

3. **Parents will act with the highest class possible in all situations.** This means no yelling at players, coaches, or officials. You may not realize this, but it *embarrasses* your kid. Every athletic event should be a positive experience for every player, coach, official, *and* parent.

When was the last time you applauded officials and thanked them for their service? Let's make it a point to treat officials with the respect they deserve.

4. **Parents will allow their children to face adversity.** Athletic seasons are long and unpredictable. There will be good days and there will be bad days. Your son/daughter will never play enough nor be happy every second. Always be a supporter, but do not always try to be the problem-solver. Let your child face adversity. Perseverance is one of the greatest attributes sports can teach athletes.

Inside the Huddle
As a parent, which one of these creeds is most difficult to follow? Why is that?

Executing the Play
Designate someone who will hold you accountable to the "Youth Sports Parent Athletic Creed" ...and make sure you hold someone else accountable.

WHAT REALLY DRIVES RESULTS

Imagine this: You are the best player on a basketball team that just won a huge game to advance in the state tournament. Visibly upset, you abruptly leave the locker room as your team celebrates. Why? You shot 1 for 8 from the field and only scored 3 points while a handful of college scouts witnessed from the stands.

Imagine this: You just lost 6-0, 6-0 in your conference tennis tournament, but minutes later you find out your team claimed its first conference championship in 25 years. Instead of celebrating, you isolate yourself from the team because lamenting your loss is more important to you than your team's accomplishments.

Imagine this: You just coached your team to its first district championship in the last fifteen years but when you get home, you are greeted with an email from a disgruntled parent over his child's lack of playing time.

All of these stories are real and, unfortunately, they occur at alarming rates. It is easy to blame kids for their selfish behavior or their parents for allowing it to happen, but we can't. This is a societal problem, not a kid or parent problem. Everywhere we look we find another online post about how great our kids are performing. Highlight films are created for elementary-age children in hopes that a college recruiter will see them. In many cases, "I" has become more important than "we."

In my own home, I have made the mistake of asking these two questions after my kids played a basketball game: "Did your team win?" followed by "How many points did you score?" I immediately made individual performance just as important as team performance. To make matters worse, if they told me they did not score at all, I would ask, "How many times did you shoot?" and "How many minutes did you play?"

Talk about setting my children up for failure.

It's no wonder that more kids struggle with anxiety today than ever before. We live in a culture driven by results. But while results and success certainly have their places, at what point must we turn our attention to the process instead of the end product?

Well, what can we control? While we can't always control the end product, we can control the process. We cannot control our playing time, points scored, hits in a baseball game, kills in volleyball, or goals scored in soccer, but we can control the hard work, discipline, and commitment that we invest into our sport. In order to initiate a cultural shift, our focus needs to be on character skills, not performance skills and outcomes.

Do you think your daughter would become a better player if she just focused on hard work, discipline, and commitment? The answer is a resounding "Yes!"

Do you think your son would become a better teammate if he just focused on hard work, discipline, and commitment? Again, the answer would be a resounding "Yes!"

Athletes' development can be stunted by their fixation on numbers. Some get so caught up in statistics that they forget what it takes to improve. They never get better. Their confidence diminishes and their attitudes sour, and the resulting impact is significant for the individual and the team.

A growth mindset approach can create a positive culture, within which all members of a team will be motivated by each teammate's improvement. Don't worry about the numbers, just pay attention to the character values that *lead to* results. Toward the end of every day, ask your kids how they did with their moral skills. Ask them if they were good teammates? These factors will lead to a success you never imagined, creating healthier, happier children who will be more motivated than ever. As parents, we have an immense responsibility to encourage a shift in those cultural values and to turn our focus toward skills consisting of high morals, high character, and integrity.

Imagine this: You get cut as a junior from the volleyball team but instead of dwelling on what society might deem a failure, you are determined to focus on discipline and hard work. The next year you try out again and not only do you make the team, but you eventually receive an offer to play at the collegiate level. Your primary focus was never on making the team or playing in college, it was striving to get better every day through discipline and hard work. High moral and character skills will win every time.

Inside the Huddle
What is the first thing you ask your child after a contest? Is the question about something he or she can control?

Executing the Play
List three different areas of your life that, as parents, you can control when it comes to youth sports. Have your kids do the same for their respective roles. Your focus during the course of your current or upcoming season needs to be centered around these three controllable areas.

30 Second Timeout

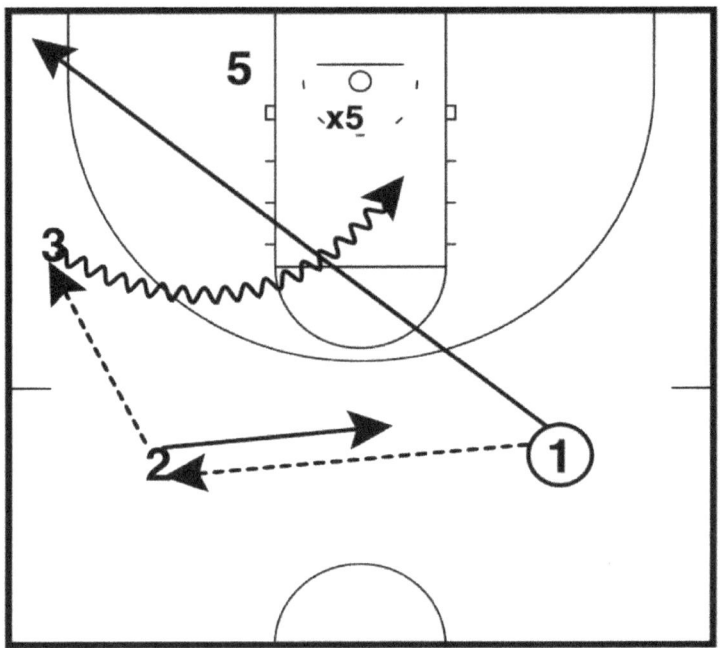

CAN WE TEACH SPORTSMANSHIP?

"A poorly officiated game lends itself to bad sportsmanship."

I received this comment from one parent after a contest in which many penalties were called. My first thought after hearing this was how easy it is to use officiating as an excuse for behaviors occurring throughout the course of a game. Upon further reflection I realized that, unfortunately, this parent's comment contained some truth.

Time and time again, we see how coaches and players react to what they feel are bad calls. We have witnessed rough games in which players are on the edge of "dirty" play, often accompanied by inappropriate "trash" talk to opponents and sometimes even officials. While we can acknowledge that this happens, it does not make these actions acceptable. The question we must then ask is this: Do we intentionally teach sportsmanship or do we just expect that our student-athletes know what it means?

By definition, sportsmanship is the fair and generous behavior or treatment of others, especially in a sports contest. The key word in that definition is "behavior." Our behavior is ultimately our choice. In order to display proper behavior in adverse situations, we must develop a moral intelligence. Moral intelligence is simply the values that make up our character. In a contest which begins to unravel, not all participants become emotionally unstable. In fact, most players, through the adversity, act with high character and integrity. Those athletes choose to do the right thing because they have developed a moral compass derived from their values. Athletes who have yet to establish values do not know how to act in those situations and have a tendency for letting their emotions get the best of them.

The question then becomes, "How do we teach sportsmanship?" As adults, our first task is to model the behavior. I attend many games where the coaches negatively yell at the officials. This, in turn, riles up the crowd and eventually rubs off on the athletes on the field. Negativity breeds negativity. In sports without officials, adult spectators can be even more at fault for creating a negative environment when their comments are heard by their child's actual opponents. On the golf course, I have witnessed parents intimidate opponents by how close they stand to them or by making noise during shots. And in tennis, I have witnessed parents cheering opponents' mistakes or calling balls in and out for their son or daughter, a job strictly for the participants. What we model as parents enhances the behavior athletes exhibit during the course of competition.

The next step to intentionally teaching sportsmanship is openly talking about this subject at home: discussing firsthand positive examples of sportsmanship while also discussing instances of poor behavior. With these examples, we can challenge our kids with different scenarios and discuss how they would respond to them. While sitting at the dinner table, we can present our children with hypothetical situations: What would you do if someone spit in your face? What would you do if someone called you a racial slur? Or, what would you do if you knew your opponent was cheating during the competition?

All of these scenarios are real, so having a course of action *before* they occur will prepare our sons and daughters to act accordingly with moral intelligence. Values are developed through these very important conversations at home.

The world offers many positive stories of sportsmanship, yet on a daily basis, a growing number of poor decisions occur in youth sports and beyond. Sportsmanship is a behavior that requires an action. Each action requires a choice. What choices are we going to make that will allow our kids to grow and be transformed by the sports they choose to play? By making the right choice, we can also ensure that the environment at each event is a positive one for the players, coaches, officials, and spectators. Yes, we can teach sportsmanship! Let's all make the right choice!

Inside the Huddle
Ask your child to recall a time when he or she witnessed a positive sportsmanship moment as well as a moment of poor sportsmanship.

Executing the Play
Define the number one value you would like your child to practice when playing sports. Give examples of what that value would look like on the playing field.

30 Second Timeout

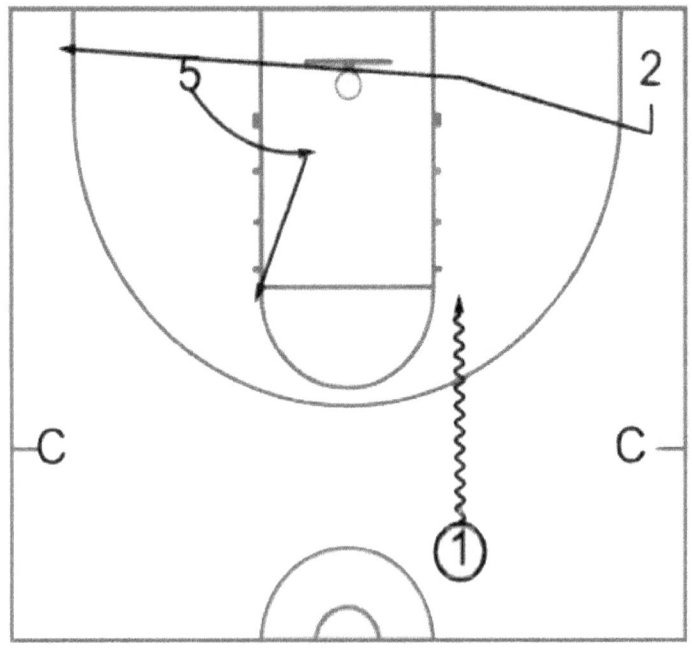

WHEN TIME STANDS STILL

After hiking 5.5 miles with a 2,000 foot elevation gain, we finally reached Amphitheater Lake in the Grand Tetons. The day could not have been more perfect: 70 degrees and brilliant blue skies, yet snow still blanketed the sides of the mountains. As we sat on one of the massive boulders overlooking this lake, my lone thought was, *If I could only freeze this moment in time*. Nobody wanted to leave. Last spring break I had the same thought as the sun set over the Seven Mile Bridge in the Florida Keys, my wife and I sitting poolside while watching our kids swim. And just this past summer I enjoyed a similar experience, gathered among family and friends around a beach bonfire in Glen Arbor. Scarcely a ripple creased the surface of Lake Michigan.

The grandeur, beauty, and serenity of these moments will never be forgotten, but the real reason I wanted them to stand forever still is that I was able to share them with my family.

The sad reality is that we all have shared times like these in our lives, only to have them quickly expire when we return to the "rat race" back at home. Many of your calendars probably look very similar to ours: Monday practice, Tuesday game, Wednesday dance, Thursday another game, Friday practice, then three more games over the weekend. Before we know it, Monday is here to start all over again.

Busyness is a disease, a vicious cycle which creates two deficiencies within people: stress and entitlement. Since 2007, the American Psychological Association has published an annual survey concerning stress in America. Year after year the survey concludes that the underlying cause of stress is busyness. The busier we are, the greater the chance of irritability, anxiety, insomnia, and fatigue. This all spills over into the relationships and partnerships we have with coaches, friends, and even our own families.

Busyness also encourages entitlement. Entitlement is a silent killer of athletic teams; often, we are so consumed in finding more ways to raise the status of our kids, we do not even notice our actions. Instead of looking at how privileged our kids *are* with the opportunities they *have*, we simply expect that the *more* they are involved, the *more* they should get back in return.

Why am I writing this? I cannot tell you how many times over the past twenty years I have heard from parents after graduation about how fast the time goes. They feel those precious years were wasted by overscheduling activities and worrying about things they could not control: making the team, playing time, college scholarships. The answer is not simple because we all realize that travel sports and offseason training are not going away. We still want all of our student-athletes to maximize their potential, and youth athletics continues to teach some of life's greatest lessons.

Can there be a balance? Can we slow down just enough to recognize those timeless moments in our lives? Can we create more opportunities for time to stand still? Can we worry a little less while gaining a broader perspective, minimizing those feelings of entitlement?

I don't know my son's batting average last summer or the record my daughter earned in tennis, but I will never forget all of us sitting on a boulder 10,000 feet above sea level, looking down on crystal blue water, recounting the journey that led us there. My guess is that my wife, son, and two daughters will never forget that moment, either. Remember this sentiment from writer Bill Keane: "Yesterday is history, tomorrow is a mystery, today is a gift of God, which is why we call it the present." Slow down and enjoy the journey while embracing every moment.

Let time stand still.

Inside the Huddle
When was the last time you experienced a "timeless" moment with your family? What was it?

Executing the Play
List ways your family can capture more "timeless" moments over the next year.

30 Second Timeout

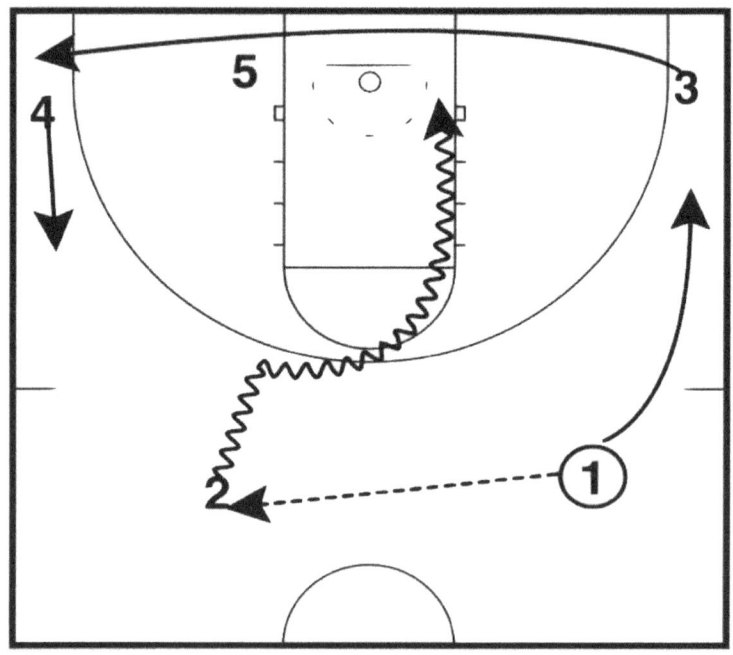

PARENT COACH

"Come on, buddy! How many times have I told you to get your hands through quicker! Don't bail out with your front foot. Get into a more athletic position!"

The more I coached my son in the art of hitting, the more discouraged he became. It seemed like every time we went to the ball field to practice, we both left upset. I felt so frustrated because all I ever tried to do was coach my son, help him get better. I've coached seemingly countless kids from five-year-olds to elite varsity athletes in various sports over eighteen years and forty-plus seasons. Why are *my* kids not receptive to my advice and teaching? They should feel lucky to have a dad with so much experience in this area.

Right?

After leaving the ball fields on one particular night, I began to do some serious self-evaluation on the matter. Am I putting too much pressure on my kids to succeed? It's easy to do when we look at the numbers: Around five percent of the boys in his class will make a basketball team in high school, while around seven percent will make a baseball team. Those percentages are sliced in half when we start talking about making a varsity team.

Then it hit me: My son does not need a coach for a dad. He needs *Dad*.

More than anything, my son loves to fish. Where did that come from? We go out fishing a few times every summer, but by no means am I an avid fisherman or outdoorsman. I am a coach who spends the little free time I have watching and playing sports. How can my son like fishing so much? Then I realized it is the one thing we do together in which I give no advice and I don't coach; the two of us simply create a lot of great memories. My son feels no pressure when we fish--it's just a dad and his son sitting in a boat waiting for the next fish to be caught, talking about whatever comes to their minds.

I have learned two lessons from this experience. The first is that our own passion does not always translate into our kids' passion. That is why it is so important to expose our kids to many different things at a young age. Music, art, sports... You may be surprised at the things they find interesting and enjoy.

The second lesson I've learned as a parent is to make other sports like fishing: no advice, no coaching. If you are pitching baseballs, make a game out of it, like Home Run Derby. If you are playing basketball, play PIG or HORSE. Even better, organize a 2-on-2 basketball or some wiffle ball with the neighbor kids. Fun at an early age equals passion. Passion will produce work ethic. Work ethic will produce results.

Despite the fact that, as parents, we want to control so much of our kids' experiences, in essence, most of their growth occurs away from us. As parents we need to encourage, support, and love our kids unconditionally. I'll bet that if I back off my son and just *play* sports with him rather than *coach* him, he will, at some point, come to me and ask for advice. Not an easy task considering the competitive environment we are a part of, but a task worth working at. I can coach forever, but I only have one shot at being a dad.

Fast forward: I wrote this "30 Second Timeout" article eight years ago when my son was ten years old. He is now going to graduate from high school and he never did play baseball or basketball beyond his sophomore year. However, that worked out well because he ultimately played tennis and ran track. Starting to play one sport when we are young does not necessarily mean that we will still play it in high school. Always keep the door open to different opportunities.

Oh, I almost forgot to mention that he still loves to fish.

Inside the Huddle
Have you ever coached your son or daughter in a sport? What made that experience rewarding? What made that experience challenging?

Executing the Play
Have your kids invite some of their friends over for a neighborhood game of kickball, wiffleball, basketball--or whatever else you can think of--that they can play simply for the fun of the game.

30 Second Timeout

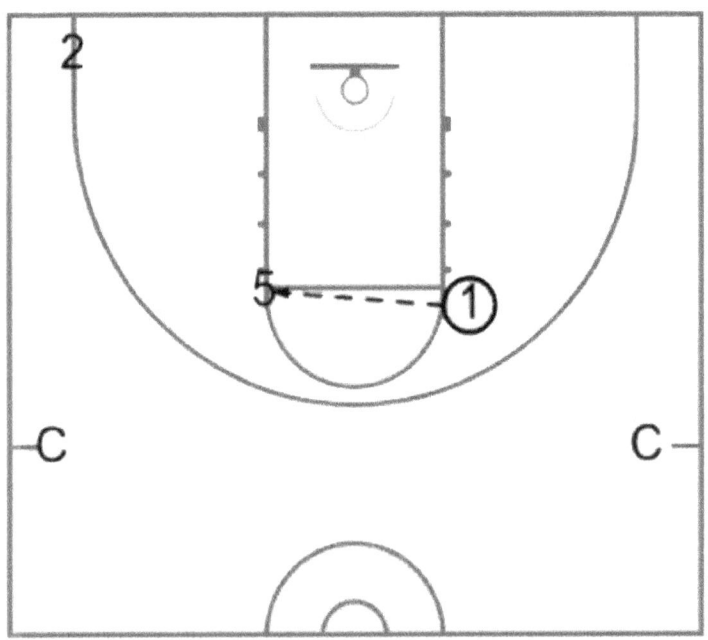

PLEASE OPEN THE DOOR

Why do kids stop playing sports?

This question has been asked repeatedly over the past few years. A number of recent studies indicate that 70% of kids stop playing sports by the age of thirteen. This can be attributed to several factors including burnout, demanding parents, and an overemphasis on winning by coaches of young athletes. Also, the natural attrition that occurs as kids enter high school plays a role in the significant decline of sports participation after the age thirteen.

I believe the answer goes even deeper than these reasons.

As parents, we are the first to expose our kids to athletics. Naturally, we tend to encourage our sons and daughters to play the same sports we participated in when we were young. Past experience playing a particular sport gives us as parents the confidence and skill set to teach our kids. And as parents, our hope is that our children find the same passion or success we'd had when we played that sport. However, after years of participation, some kids may never develop that same level of passion, or they might find themselves lacking the skills to make a high school team. Consequently, it is easy to put all of our eggs in a couple of baskets, limiting opportunities in other areas where our kids may have strengths.

As a father with two children now in high school, I will offer my own experience as an example. I became a sports fanatic at a young age, playing basketball, tennis, and baseball whenever the opportunity presented itself. When our twins were two years old, I put a cement slab in our backyard with a basketball hoop because I assumed they would be basketball players like my wife and I were in high school.

Neither of our twins played basketball after tenth grade. That cement slab now holds our trampoline.

My oldest daughter had a tennis racket in her hands by the age of five. Years later, when she considered going out for the golf team her freshman year, my initial reaction was, "She can't play golf!" Why would I think this and why would I care how good she would be or not? The reason is that as parents, we often times put up barriers because we feel that trying something new may impede further development in the sports they are currently playing. Too often as parents, we put blinders on and only recognize certain sports because they were the ones *we* played or because we believe they are the only sports that matter. I'm thankful that my daughter decided to play golf. She loves it and we now realize how cool it is that she is learning a sport she can play for the rest of her life.

As a high school athletic director, I have often seen kids give up on sports due to a negative experience or not making a team. When this happens, we have to realize that when one door closes, others are waiting to open. I encourage all parents to recognize the opportunity to open these doors and allow our kids to explore. We don't know what hidden talents and passions are ready to be revealed. We may find that these passions are not even centered around athletics. They may come in the form of the arts or maybe even service opportunities that will benefit others. As parents, let's take off those blinders and listen to what our kids might be trying to tell us. They could be offering us the insight needed to uncover hidden talents we never knew existed.

Inside the Huddle
Are the sports your kids play the same as those you played when you were young? Have you ever encouraged your son or daughter to try something in which you have no experience? What are the rewards and challenges of both?

Executing the Play
Expand other opportunities for your kids to explore. If they are younger, put them in a different sport or activity to see if a passion develops. If they are older and a door closes on one opportunity, involve them in something else.

30 Second Timeout

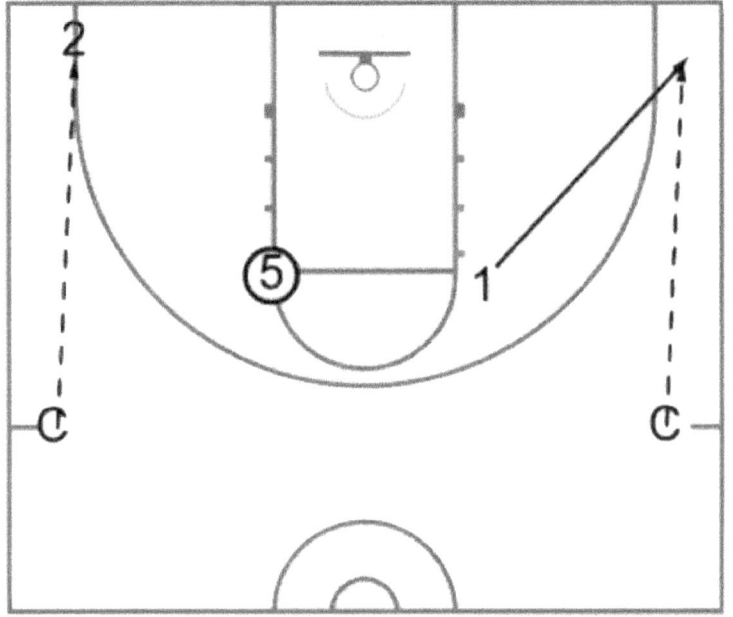

COACHING FROM THE STANDS

I love the game of basketball, so when given the opportunity to break away from my job, I would go and watch my nephew play on the east side of the state. As I settled in the bleachers on one winter evening, I noticed how jovial people were around me. Laughter filled the air as they talked about the upcoming holidays and whatever else was on their minds.

Then came "The Star-Spangled Banner."

Have you ever noticed how the atmosphere changes after the national anthem? Laughter stops. Side conversations stop. Anxiety, tension, and the overall intensity in the gym changes in a matter of moments. The same people who were so relaxed and happy ten minutes earlier are now yelling at officials and telling their son or daughter what to do on the court.

"Parent of Athlete Syndrome" has set in.

Anyone with a child who plays sports at any level has experienced this phenomenon. Something inside of us changes when the game begins. Some describe this as a "beast" that emerges while our child competes. Our brains lose rational thinking and we say things we know we should not say, but we can't control it. Over the years, I have known so many parents who've wished they would have kept silent and just enjoyed the moment while their child was playing.

We have an opportunity to learn from those lessons and, in return, change a negative athletic culture into something positive: a culture in which student-athletes can grow, develop, and become the best they can be.

Parents cross the boundaries of their defined role when they yell from the stands at their kids to do certain things. Coaches coach, parents parent (support) and players play. I have observed this "coaching in the stands," at about every level of every sport. I have observed a little league parent telling her son to shift in the outfield when the coaches wanted everyone moving up because the batter was bunting. As a golf coach, I have observed a dad telling his daughter with hand signals what club she should use on her next shot. How many times have we been to a basketball game and heard someone shout "Shoot it" or "Take it to the rack"?

Coaching from the sidelines can also carry over to the car ride home and dominate dinner table conversations. We do this because we love our kids and want the best for them. However, coaching from the sidelines creates a confusing situation for athletes because they are getting mixed messages. The coach is saying one thing and the "coach" in the stands is saying another. If you want your children to be the best they can be, encourage them to listen to one voice: their coach's.

The next time you are sitting in the stands and you feel the "beast" approaching, stay calm, keep silent, and enjoy the moment. Remember how much of a privilege it is for your child to be a part of an athletic team and how quickly the time will pass. And enjoy the ride.

Inside the Huddle
What is the difference between "cheering for" and "coaching" your child from the stands?

Executing the Play
If you find yourself wanting to coach your son or daughter during a game, try to move farther away from the playing field.

CHASING AFTER THE WIND

Wind.

We hear this word in many different phrases. When you want someone to run fast, you will tell them to run *like the wind*. When you take a risk in life without worrying about negative results, you may find yourself throwing caution *to the wind*. Other times in our lives, when something disappears forever, we may say it is gone *with the wind*. What do you think about when you hear the phrase, "Chasing after the wind"? In the literal sense, "chasing after the wind" is an impossible task because the goal is to capture whatever you are chasing. The next time you are outside, try to capture the wind with your hands. It's impossible.

How often, as parents, do we "chase after the wind" in regard to our child's involvement with youth/high school sports?

I remember when our twins were born; one of the first gifts we gave them was a Little Tikes basketball hoop. They could barely even hold a ball, let alone shoot it. But I had no doubt that eventually they would be good. They had no choice. Their dad was the varsity basketball coach and since basketball was my vocational identity, surely basketball would become their identities as well. Now as seniors in high school, neither of them play. I was "chasing after the wind."

As a 22-year-old varsity basketball coach, I felt as if the sky was the limit: Conference, District, Regional, and State Championships were all going to be a part of my Hall of Fame career. Nine years later, I was not coaching high school basketball any longer. Again, I found myself "chasing after the wind." Not until my kids were older did I realize that overstressing performance was no different than "chasing after the wind." The same can be said of the latter part of my coaching career, when I realized the performance of my teams was also like "chasing after the wind." An athlete may have a tremendous work ethic but still get beat out for a spot on the team because someone else, who also works hard, has superior skills.

Just one injury can derail an athletic career to a point that the athlete may never play at the same level again, if at all. Multiple injuries on a talented team may shatter championship dreams. Sometimes, our expectations for our kids are unrealistic and can never be achieved. Performance and results may be impossible to capture due to many uncontrollable variables--much like "chasing after the wind."

What if we stopped "chasing after the wind" and began to "catch the wind?" By simply changing one word we change the entire meaning of the phrase. "Catching the wind" means to gain knowledge or a better understanding of something. Our kids may be outperformed by a better player, become injured, or fail to live up to our expectations; each of these can present to us both knowledge and areas in which to grow. Attitude, integrity, grit, perseverance, and work ethic are all behaviors that *can* be controlled and developed by everyone.

Every outcome that occurs in sports presents to us an opportunity to "catch the wind." Think how much more enjoyable navigating through youth sports would be if we just took the time to "catch the wind" rather than "chasing after the wind." Seventy percent of kids quit sports before the age of thirteen. It is no longer fun, and the reason it is no longer fun is that performance standards have become more important than learned behaviors. Looking back, did I emphasize performance too much with my own kids in regard to basketball? Is that why they are not playing anymore? As parents, we have only one shot at making this experience a positive one for them.

"Catching the wind" has taken a backseat to "chasing the wind." Think of our kids as kites: When we hang on tight and allow the kite to catch the wind, it creates an adventurous but exhilarating experience with no regrets. When we let go of the kite and chase after it, the end result will be that the kite will crash and become destroyed. Now is the time to hang on tight and enjoy the ride. No more chasing after the wind.

Inside the Huddle
How do you choose to "catch the wind" instead of "chasing after the wind?"

Executing the Play
Develop a list of behaviors your child can control in regard to playing sports. Define these behaviors by how they could look on the playing field.

30 Second Timeout

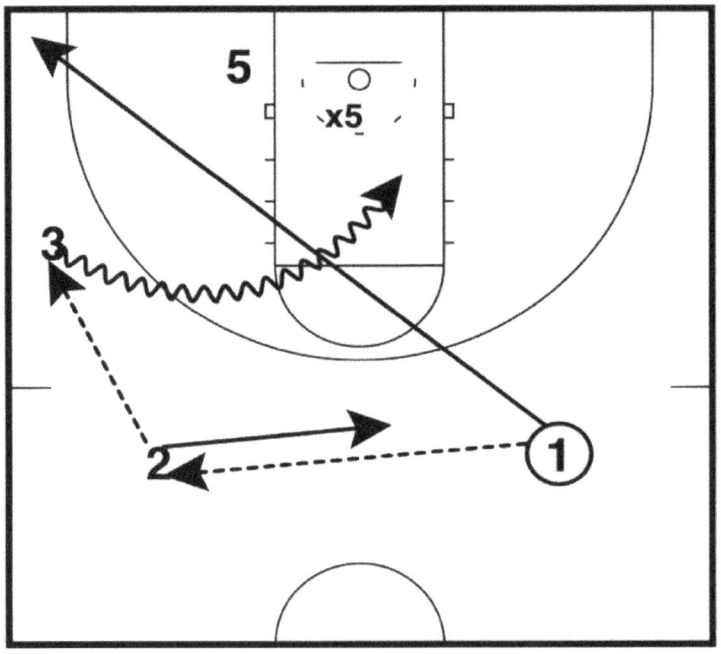

WHAT DO YOU STAND FOR?

As I was walking out of the gym after a volleyball tournament, I couldn't help but overhear a conversation between a father and his daughter who'd just played in the championship game.

"Could you hear me in the stands?" asked the dad.

"Yes," she replied.

"Did I pump you guys up?" he asked.

With a smile on her face, the daughter answered, "Yes, Dad. You pumped us up."

Her dad went on to say, "I just wanted to go out there and spike a volleyball on someone." He proceeded to demonstrate the action in front of his daughter.

On the brink of laughter, the daughter chuckled, "Probably not a good idea, Dad!"

After a long pause, he told her, "I love to watch you play!"

Sheepishly, she responded back, "Thanks for coming today, Dad!"

That young lady's feelings about playing high school sports had just been elevated by her parent's one simple sentence.

Shortly after witnessing that conversation, an opposing school's athletic director forwarded me a message from a couple of our parents who were very complimentary about their school and the sportsmanship they'd demonstrated on the field. As an athletic director and coach, these moments validate for me the positive culture that the opposing school is trying to instill. Athletics have become more and more "Win at all costs," so to see parents acknowledge another school is refreshing.

At a soccer game this fall, I was walking an official to his car when a parent greeted the official at the gate and genuinely thanked him for his efforts on a job well done. Hearing so many negative stories regarding youth sports across America, it is inspiring to witness these positive interactions between father-daughter, parent-opposing school, and parent-official.

As parents and spectators, in order to create a positive culture within our programs, we must ask ourselves, "What do we stand for?" If you can truly answer this question honestly, it will help guide every conversation you have with your child, as well as every reaction you have toward officials, coaches, and opposing teams. What *you* stand for and how that is portrayed will impact your child in ways you would never imagine, now and in the future.

If we yell at officials, all we are doing is teaching our impressionable youth that this behavior is acceptable. When our kids become parents themselves, all we'll have taught them is that it is ok to berate officials when they think a mistake has been made. Is this what we stand for? The same can be said when, in front of our kids, we negatively talk about people associated with athletics, whether they are members of our child's team, coaches, or opposing teams. Is this what we stand for?

As a parent, it becomes very easy to find myself wrapped up in the emotions surrounding the sports my own kids play. Bad calls by officials, frustration in our child's performance, and lack of playing time can all lead to the potential for negative responses. So how do we remain positive during these adverse situations?

It goes back to those values you established by asking the core question, "What do I stand for?" I presented this challenge to our coaching staff and I am going to present the same challenge to every parent of an athlete: See how often you can recognize something positive and let that individual or team know through an email, letter, or simply by saying "Thank you" or "Good job." By doing this, we can all take part in creating a positive culture while modeling what it is we stand for.

Inside the Huddle:
What values are important in your family? For you as a parent, how do those values carry over into the athletic arena?

Executing the Play
Over the course of the next season, make it a point to thank your coaches for all the time and commitment they put into their teams while also thanking officials for their efforts at a particular competition.

30 Second Timeout

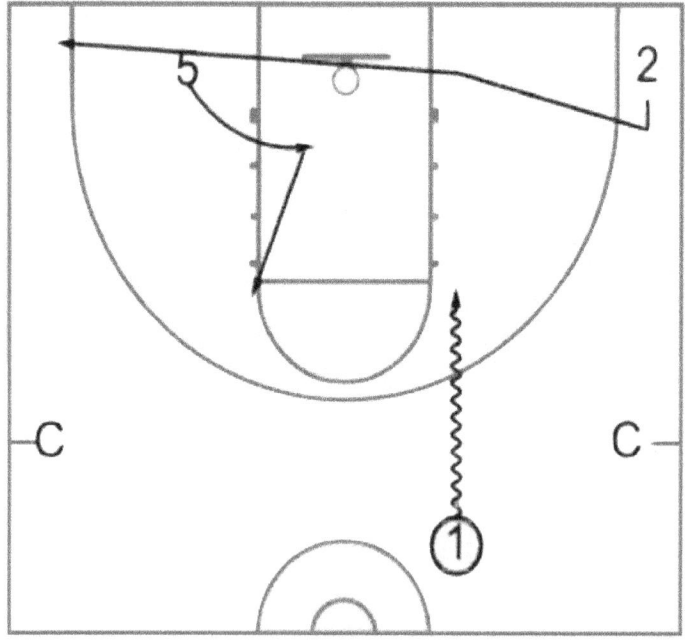

WHAT CAN WE LEARN FROM A 4TH GRADE TEACHER?

The end of an elementary school year is not complete without Field Day. Students compete to see who can run the fastest, throw the farthest, and jump rope the longest. However, the highlight of the 4th/5th grade Field Day is the Tug o' War competition. Grade levels from all of the elementary schools in the district compete against each other to see who has the strongest class.

When my youngest daughter was in 4th grade, her class won the Tug o' War event, but that is irrelevant in comparison to what Mr. Kooiker told his students after it was finished. Amid all of the screaming and unbridled excitement, Mr. Kooiker said something my daughter will never forget: "Class, we did not win because of the people who were tugging. We won because of how the rest of the classmates were cheering. When times were tough and the tuggers wanted to quit, you would not let them through your continuous encouragement!"

Six boys and six girls were selected to comprise their Tug o' War team. This left the other fifteen students with a decision to make: They could either feel sorry for themselves because they'd not been chosen or they could leave those feelings behind and cheer on their classmates. Simply put, those students could be self-serving or they could place their classmates ahead of themselves. Mr. Kooiker could have shined the spotlight on the twelve students who were assigned to be on the rope, but instead he taught a valuable lesson that day:

On any team or in any organization, every role is important, regardless of how insignificant that role may seem.

The running back who runs for 100 yards cannot do this without the help of his offensive line, just like a basketball player who scores 30 points cannot do that without assists from teammates. An all-state wrestler cannot accomplish his goals without the other members of his weight class pushing him every day in practice. How did Mr. Kooiker successfully create a positive culture in his classroom? He did this not only by cultivating relationships among the students but also by having an extraordinary ability to personally connect with each and every one of them himself.

Understanding that all roles are essential to any program's success is not all we learned from Mr. Kooiker that day. He also reminded us of the importance of encouragement and how this can create a contagious positive culture. Encouragement can occur at home between parent and athlete after a poor performance in a losing effort. Moving forward, the parent's words will have a profound effect on the athlete, as they can either infuse confidence or deepen discouragement.

Encouragement can also be pivotal on any team. Jealousy among teammates is becoming more apparent as competition for playing time grows increasingly fierce. Instead of supporting each other, some players hope for others to fail as it may benefit them. On successful teams, the athletes do not care who gets the credit and all players and coaches encourage each other. On those teams, winning is more important than individual accomplishments and playing time.

Thanks, Mr. Kooiker, for reminding us of two very important principles that can guide us within our teams, families, and jobs. Yes, we all can learn something from a 4th grade teacher!

Inside the Huddle
Why can it be difficult to recognize the bench player and the importance of his or her role?

Executing the Play
Discuss the impact of every role on your child's teams. Next, determine which role your child plays on the teams. Discuss specifically what your child can do, with his or her given role, to help the team.

30 Second Timeout

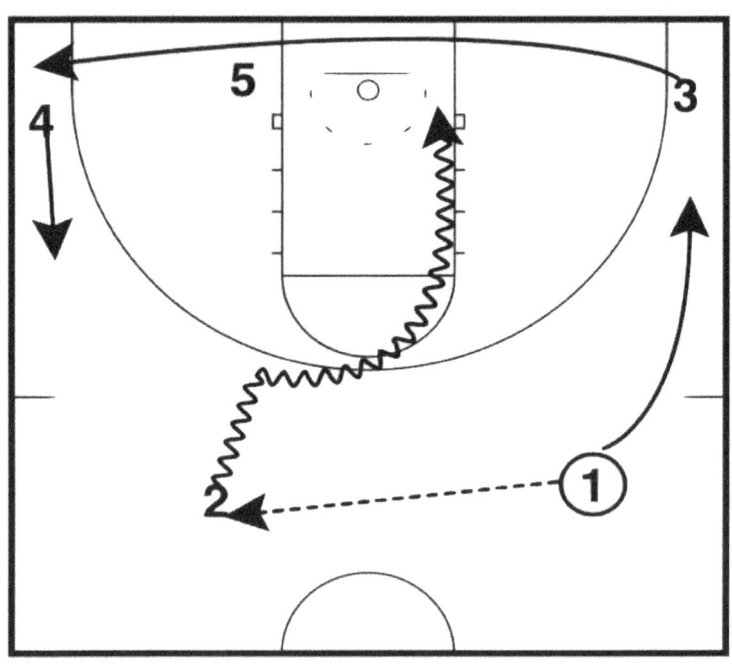

CUTS

I remember it like it was yesterday--all I could think about during the school day was basketball tryouts that night. What were we going to do? How was I going to play? How many players would they keep? What if I didn't make the team? Later, I could feel my body shaking when I dressed and entered the gym. I was so afraid of committing the one mistake that could be the difference between making the team or not. This feeling clung to me throughout every day until the coach finally posted the list. I'd made it this time. However, that anxiety would return to me for every single future tryout.

Ten years later I found myself in a different role. Now 23 and coaching varsity basketball, I was encountering many of the same feelings I'd had when trying out for my own middle school teams. Am I going to make the right decision? How many players will I keep? With twenty boys and only fifteen roster spots, it was inevitable that I would be ending the playing careers for a few student-athletes. So many of those players had put in countless hours practicing and had been playing organized basketball for years. Ultimately, I was the one who would have to tell a few of them that they were not quite good enough to be on our team anymore. I was so razzed by "cuts" that first year, I accidently told *sixteen* players they'd made the team.

After realizing my mistake, I was in a panic about what to do. Fortunately, the player whom I felt was sixteenth was relieved to know that I had made a mistake and he was content with not being a part of the team. He explained that the only reason he'd tried out in the first place was that his dad promised to buy him a pool table. True story! *Whew.* If you were to ask any coach to identify the worst couple days of the year, without hesitation the response would be "Tryouts." Coaches begin coaching because of a passion for working with kids and they want to use the sport they love as a way to give back. They do not get into coaching because they want to cut kids and tell them they can't be a part of something.

Move the clock ahead another twenty years: Now, I am a parent of kids who will soon experience their first tryout for their high school teams. I have pitched countless balls, fed thousands of tennis balls, and I have rebounded an endless number of shots taken in the gym.

As dedicated parents of young athletes, that is why it is only natural to feel like we are trying out when our children are trying out. What if he or she doesn't make the team? How are people going to perceive *me* if my kid does not make it, and does that mean I have failed as a parent? Some people may not ask the same questions, but all parents will feel some sort of anxiety going into tryouts because we love our kids and do not want to see them hurting.

These emotions are real and no matter what I write, they will never go away. Hopefully, this article will offer you a bit of perspective along with some healthy ways to deal with your son or daughter not making a team.

One word describes what all athletes, coaches, and parents feel during tryouts: Worry. You might be surprised to learn that a recent University of Cincinnati study found that 85% of what we worry about never happens.

> "Why worry about things you can't control when you can keep yourself busy controlling the things that depend on you?"
> ~John C. Maxwell

We can control our effort, how well we prepare, and the positive thoughts we put into our heads, but we cannot control everything we worry about. As athletes, we cannot worry about what people are going to say if we don't make the team. Parents should not worry about where they stand in the sports hierarchy if their son or daughter gets cut. The reason we do not need to worry is that at the end of the day, sports can never define a person. If we allow sports to define who we are in high school, then what happens when our playing days are over? How are we defined then? Clearly, sports play a pivotal role in developing beneficial life skills for athletes as they move on from high school, but they are not the only means for developing those skills.

The following are some guidelines for parents to follow to help them use tryouts and cuts as valuable learning experiences:

Be sensitive in how you react to finding out your son or daughter was "cut."
>If you become emotional about the situation and get upset in front of your child, you are modeling how to react when adversity strikes. The two most important things a parent can do in this situation is to listen and be empathetic.

Release your child to the problem.
>Your child will be upset if he or she does not make a team. As parents, we want to fix our child's problem, but we must remember that we are not the one trying out. The role of parents in this situation is to help their child through the process. Provide insight on how to address the coach about the reason for being cut or ask about areas that could be worked on if planning to try out again next year.

Reinforce that even though your child did not make a team, he or she is not a failure.
>As a parent, this is a great opportunity to share with your child failures you have experienced in your own life. Then, note that how we respond to failure speaks more about our character than anything else. Also, encourage your child to hold onto his or her dreams. You can find so many stories of people who have experienced failure and used that failure as motivation to achieve success later in life.

How should athletes respond to being cut? The first thing they need to realize is that everyone fails--especially when risks are taken. We all know that trying out for a sports team is a risk and that, in itself, should be commended. Over time, the more risks they take, the more opportunities they have for growth through failures and successes. Next, it is important to gather as much information as possible regarding their weaknesses and what they can do to strengthen them. Finally, they should never give up on their dreams.

I had a former basketball player who was cut his freshman, sophomore, and junior year. He decided to try one last time his senior year. Something about his resilience and determination made me believe he could help the team in practice. Initially, he was my 12th man but by the end of the season, he was the first guy off the bench, playing an equally important but different role on our team. That experience would not have happened if he didn't continue to try out for basketball after his freshman season. Two years after graduation, this young man was diagnosed with cancer. He met this challenge the same way he met the challenge of making the basketball team: He never gave up and he persevered through treatment to become cancer-free.

Student-athletes need to keep an open mind if they do not make the team because we all know that when one door closes, others may open with different opportunities. These opportunities could be in the same sport or something completely different. Never stop dreaming!

Inside the Huddle
Talk with your child about a time when you did not make a team or were declined for a job and how that made you feel?

Executing the Play
If your child gets cut from a team, make sure you react empathetically. Give advice on how to positively deal with the unfortunate circumstances. Don't try to fix the situation, just be there for your child and reinforce that he or she is not a failure.

WHAT HAPPENS WHEN THE GAME IS OVER?

I love playing cribbage, I think mainly because it was a game I played with my dad and brother when I was a kid. I think another reason I enjoy cribbage so much is that I win most of the time (just ask my wife). Cribbage is a game just as athletics is a game just as life is a game. So, what happens when the game is over? We will answer that question at the end, but first we need to ask, "How do we keep score?" In sports, we keep score by looking at the scoreboard. Very rarely is the result a tie, so the scoreboard does a great job of determining winners and losers. John Ortberg, in his book *It All Goes Back in the Box*, has a different idea of how people keep score: Comparison and Competition.

How often do we go and watch our kids' sporting events and start comparing them to the other kids, all the while analyzing where they fit within the sports hierarchy? When they are only eight years old, we try to figure out whether or not they will make the high school team and what position they will play. I am as guilty as anyone else of having these thoughts, but becoming an athletic director has been the best thing ever to happen to me in this area of my life. My focus is now on over 1000 student-athletes and how athletics can transform their lives, not just the three kids in our house. When we compare our kids to others, we worry. When we worry, we become stressed. When we are stressed, we will never fully enjoy the experience of having a child who participates in sports.

Competition, when used in a healthy way, is one of the reasons I love sports. Watching athletes and teams persevere through adversity is a highlight for me because I know those moments will shape them as they move forward in life. Competition becomes a problem in youth sports when parents and athletes, coveting more playing time, hope another individual performs poorly. As a coach and athletic director, I have witnessed some athletes and parents who were more concerned about individual success than whether or not the team won. This type of internal competition within a team can destroy chemistry and create a negative environment.

A few years back we had sisters who joined the basketball team late because they enrolled after practices had begun. Coaches were worried about team chemistry and how the team's roles would change. But instead of jealousy getting in the way, the team accepted these girls and their new roles. This selfless decision by the other players resulted in two of the most successful seasons in school history.

So what happens when the game is over?

At the end of day, when we are encountering death, only two things matter: the relationships we share with others and the legacy we leave. With every passing season, the athletic teams for which your children played will continue to strive for greatness and excellence in everything they do. They will celebrate team success as well as individual accomplishments. And while every instance of recognition is great, Ortberg points out that it "will all go back in the box." It's just like the last game of cribbage I played with my wife: When it was over, we put the cards back in the box and the pegs back to the start line. We stored them both in a drawer where they wait until the next time we want to play.

We all understand the significance of relationships and the effects these can have in our homes, schools, workplaces, and communities. Can you imagine the positive culture we can create if athletes and parents are more concerned about legacy than individual accomplishments? As we focus on the season in front of us, let's each place relationships and legacy in front of everything else. Some of my greatest memories as a high school athlete are products of the relationships I formed with my coaches. To this day, I regularly connect with them. Those relationships and particularly their impact--will never go back in the box.

Inside the Huddle
Why is it so hard for some athletes to move on when athletic opportunities end?

Executing the Play
As a parent, make sure your child understands that eventually, when moving on toward life's next stage, he or she will not be defined by sports. Ask this question to your son or daughter: "What do you want to be known for?"

This will help provide separation between person and sport.

30 Second Timeout

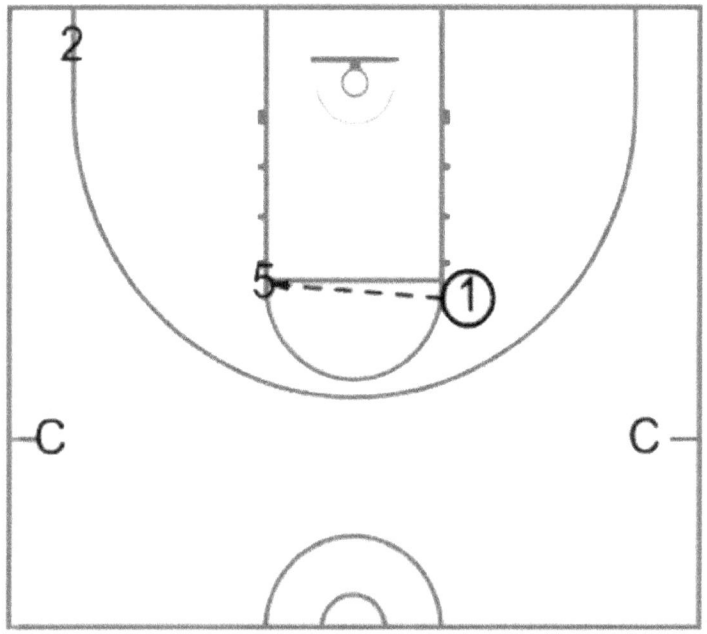

WHY SO LOUD?

Have you become *that* community?

You know, that school and community everyone talks about, the one that, from the stands, yells embarrassing and disparaging remarks to officials, coaches, and even student-athletes? That school is often talked about at the water coolers before work and at the dinner table at home. We all know which schools these are because every time we compete against them, the anticipation of obnoxious behavior supersedes the actual sporting event itself. The perception of being *that* school is often tough to break. So, I ask the question again: Has your school become that school and community?

Verbal attacks on officials, along with negative comments toward our student-athletes and coaches, have become more and more common in the stands despite the fact that most of our parents and community positively support our teams and the game itself.

We need to ask ourselves these two questions:

- Why is this happening?
- What are we going to do to stop it?

The "why" centers around winning and success: Very few of these behaviors occur when a particular crowd's team is ahead in the game or has won. This can be called the "victim" mentality. We become the "victim" when things don't go our way, whether it is a call by an official, a mistake by a player, or a decision by the coach. Being a "victim" makes for an easy excuse when the final result of a competition is something other than success or victory.

After a game this past year, I had a parent approach me and say, "Why do the calls always go against us?" Yes, we had lost the game, but the other team had twice as many calls made against them as we'd had. Sometimes, we need to acknowledge that the other team is just better. One of the biggest mistakes we make as spectators is trying to control the things that cannot be controlled. We cannot control what the official is going to call, what the student-athlete is going to do, or what the coach is going to decide. Quite simply, yelling at the officials, student-athletes, and coaches will never change the outcome of a game. Ever. Most of the time, the people being yelled at don't even hear it. A better use of that energy would be to cheer on your teams, through both success and failure, in positive ways that best represent your community.

How are we going to stop this behavior? As spectators in the crowd, we must first distinguish between the things we can and cannot control. This traces back to letting officials officiate, players play, and coach's coach. Understanding this makes the experience much more enjoyable for everyone involved. As spectators in the crowd, what else can we do to create a more positive culture within our respective programs?

It begins with each program having a group of parents who are willing to lay out expectations for behavior at games. This chapter can help create awareness, but change will only occur through the people who are actively involved in it and who are present at each game. The parents within these programs set the climate and have the ability to hold one another accountable. Parents can lay out these expectations at their preseason meetings where the other parents are visible and engaged in the conversation. Occasionally during the season, email blasts can be sent to remind parents of the expectations that were collectively discussed during those meetings. Sometimes, the most powerful voice is that of someone undergoing the same experience as you.

I witnessed firsthand the power of one parent's voice through an email sent after a series of negative events at games. The emphatically written words made an immediate impact on the culture in the stands. Our student-athletes love it when their crowd is booming at games--but only in the form of positive cheers for their efforts. If we want to initiate a seismic shift from a corrosive culture to a championship culture, it all starts in the stands. Be the difference. Make the change.

Inside the Huddle
How would you rate your community on a scale of 1-10, with 1 being the worst and 10 the best, in regard to fan behavior in the crowd.

Executing the Play
At your next parent meeting, work with the coach to devise a sportsmanship plan centered around behavioral expectations for fans and parents in the stands.

30 Second Timeout

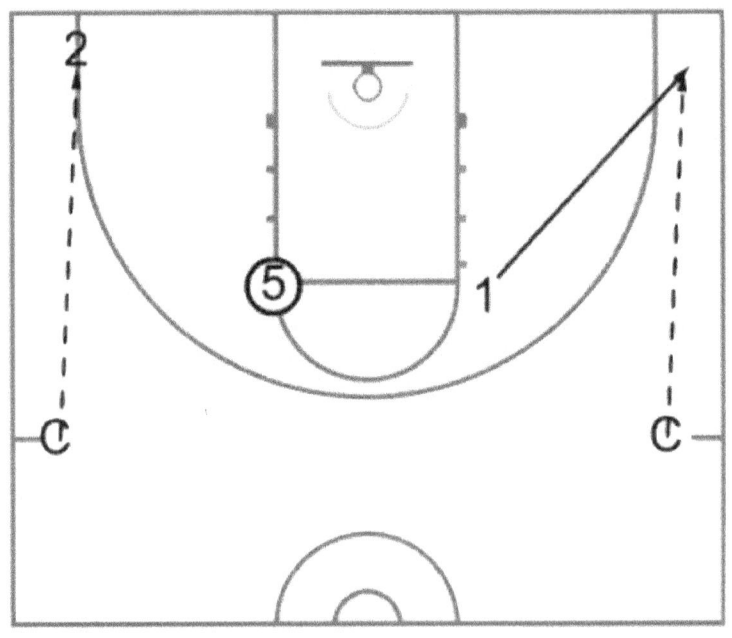

DEALING WITH THE UNEXPECTED

May 6, 1987 is a day I will never forget. After coming home from a middle school tennis match, I decided to eat a quick dinner and go to my baseball scrimmage, despite my mom saying that I should just stay home. I didn't listen to her and I arrived at the field shortly before the scrimmage began. In the second inning, as I played shortstop, an opposing batter hit a short pop fly over second base. I ran hard to make the catch while the center fielder did the same. Neither of us called off the other, resulting in a violent collision.

As the memory of that moment continues to play in slow motion, I now realize that adrenaline is capable of amazing things. After landing on the ground, I noticed how my leg had swelled up so much that it literally stretched out my sweat pants. My femur was broken. I spent six weeks in a body cast only to find out that my femur had healed incorrectly. The doctor had to break it again and start over. Despair set in, frustration spread, and anger took residence within me; I immediately became afraid that my days playing sports were over.

At this young age, a transformation slowly occurred throughout this experience: Despair was replaced by patience, frustration took a back seat to determination, and anger was displaced by perseverance as I worked extremely hard to get back onto the field. The more my leg strengthened, the more my confidence grew.

Time and time again, I have since leaned on these attributes; as a thirteen-year-old, I'd learned how to get through some extremely adverse situations. Events like these can stretch our will beyond what we ever think possible, but when people are stretched, they grow. Breaking my leg shaped the rest of my life while offering me the opportunity to find purpose and passion. Because playing sports was going to be a challenge, I knew the only way to fulfill that desire was by coaching. I started coaching tennis at sixteen years old. Through coaching, I realized how great of an impact one can have on student-athletes.

I knew before entering college that I wanted to be involved in education. Would I have felt this way if I hadn't broken my leg? I don't know. I do know, however, that when a door closes, another always opens.

The longer I have been involved with high school athletics, the more I have witnessed athletes' careers put on hold or destroyed by major injuries. For many, these injuries can cause the individual to question "What is next?" or "What am I going to do now?" Our culture has placed athletics in such high regard that when taken away, we are compelled to feel that our existence is not as valuable as it was when we were a part of them.

This transition can be difficult, often leading to feelings of low self-worth and hopelessness because athletes may feel like they have failed. For some, the failure is that they did not meet the expectations of their parents, coaches, or teammates; for others, the failure is in the realization that they could not meet their own personal goals.

Injuries are not the only cause. These feelings can also occur when a student-athlete gets cut, does not reach his or her full potential, or even when one player takes another's spot on a team. A coaching change may bring in new philosophies which may not meet certain players' skill sets, leaving those athletes sitting on the sidelines. Athletics can be unpredictable, non-forgiving, and unfair for all who participate. Because of this unpredictability, we need to prepare our kids for their lives beyond athletics. The message should be that sports will never define us, but they can prepare us for the next stages in life. Sports are not a means to an end, but rather opportunities to find our own purpose and passions. We never know in what direction certain events will lead us unless we keep an open mind and a positive attitude. If we allow them, times of adversity and transition can teach us many lessons that will play significant, positive roles in our lives.

I recently read a quote stating that the reason the windshield is bigger than the rearview mirror is that our focus should be on what is ahead of us, not what is in the past. Past experiences can prepare us for the next event, but in order to grow from those experiences, we have to keep pressing forward by looking through the windshield. Injuries can lead to opportunities, opportunities can give us a platform, and having a platform gives us the ability to impact those around us. Embrace the process!

<u>Inside the Huddle</u>
How can injuries prepare a person for life? Give some real-world examples.

<u>Executing the Play</u>
Write an encouraging note to an athlete who, due to injury, has to sit out of competition.

30 Second Timeout

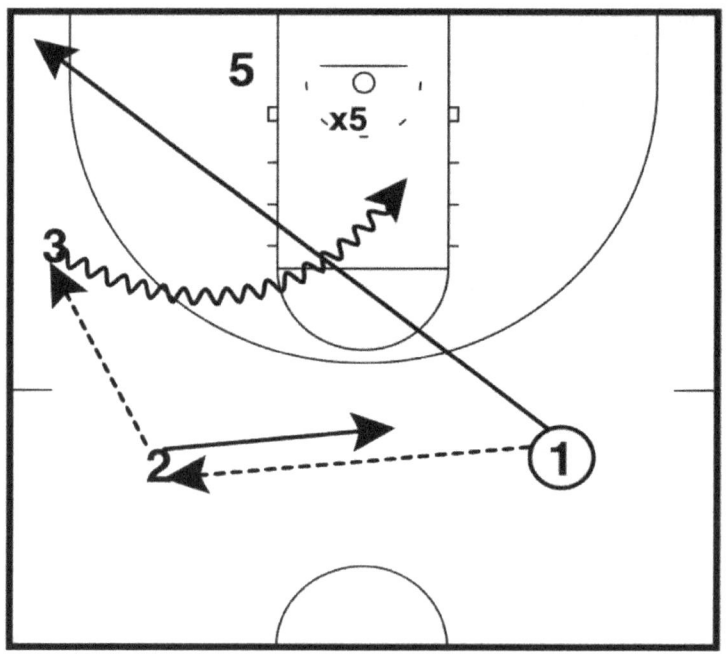

ADVERSITY

I could not wait for my junior year of playing basketball in high school. After starting every game of my freshmen and sophomore years, I was ready to be a major contributor on the varsity team. I worked hard leading up to my junior season. I spent hours in the gym, executing ball handling drills and shooting. Then I got the news.

A senior who did not play his junior year decided that he wanted to try out for the team. He was the best athlete in the senior class, starring in both football and track. I, on the other hand, after years of struggling with a severe femur break and torn cartilage in my left knee, was not nearly the athlete I once was. My deficiencies, for him, would be a strength.

The season began and I played very little while the senior athlete was consistently on the floor. How could this happen to me? I had spent hours in the gym practicing; the last time he'd picked up a ball was two years ago. The situation was not fair and I had a hard time dealing with it. What was the point of practicing hard when I knew I was not going to get into the game? At my lowest point, I learned some important lessons through very supportive parents.

My parents did not call the coach to complain. They did not sit in the stands and make excuses for why I was not playing. They told me two things that will stick with me forever. The first is that life is not always fair. They should know. My mom, who unfortunately passed away in 2019, had a condition called ataxia, a degeneration of her cerebellum, which controlled her ability to walk, talk, and utilize her muscular system. She didn't choose to be confined to a wheelchair and was frustrated with her inability to communicate. Life is not fair. The second thing my parents told me is that if I learn to work hard, at some point it always pays off. Maybe not this season or next season, but learning a positive work ethic will be a benefit to me throughout my life.

Looking back, they were right. Did I play more that season? Yes, but only because of injuries to other players. Did I have a great senior season? Not really, but I continued to put forth my best effort every day for the betterment of the team. Through these two principles I have been able to battle through four bypass surgeries in my lower leg for ongoing blood clots, while still fulfilling my dream of becoming a husband, father, teacher, coach, and athletic director.

Handling adversity is one of many great lessons taught through athletics, something that can have life-changing, transformational effects on a student-athlete. As parents, we have a tremendous opportunity to nurture our children as they face adversity. We can support them and encourage them to accept responsibility for themselves, to move forward and find solutions in positive and productive ways. As parents, we are shaping our own legacies by how we outwardly endure difficult circumstances. A time will come when, in front of your child, you are tempted to talk negatively about a coach. Or maybe you'll want to vocally blame someone else for your child's struggles. Before you speak, remember that your children will have kids of their own someday who could go through the same thing. How do you want them, as parents themselves, to react?

What is the legacy you are going to leave?

Inside the Huddle
What is the hardest thing you have had to witness your child go through? How did you work through the adversity in that situation?

Executing the Play

Stay quiet in the stands--and at home--if your child encounters adversity on the playing field.

WHAT DO YOU SAY?

"I love to watch you play."

Those are the six words every student-athlete wants to hear from his or her parents after a game. But, what if your child did *not* play? What do you say then? Parents can't say, "I love to watch you play" when their child did not make it into the game, nor can they say other post-competition statements like:

> *"Did you fight like a dog?"*
> *"Did you have fun?"*

It is hard to fight like a dog when not given the opportunity, and we all know players have more fun when they actually play in the game. If you search the phrase, "what to say after a game," Google will provide an extensive number of articles, some of them backed by research. However, when you search the phrase, "what to say when your kid does not play," Google provides far fewer. Why? This can be a difficult and very sensitive area for most parents, and it can leave them struggling to think of something appropriate and supportive.

Before we talk about what to say in response in this situation, it may be more important to discuss what *not* to say after a game in which your child did not play. Some of the comments all parents should avoid are:

> *"Why have you not played in the last three games? Your coach must not like you for some reason."*

"Your coach is clueless. He has no idea what he is doing."

"You are way better than Johnny! I can't believe he is playing more minutes than you."

"Did you see how many mistakes Suzie made? I know if you were given the opportunity, you would not make those same mistakes."

Parents will often say these things because they are frustrated and they think that they are comforting their child by providing excuses. What these comments actually do is create a divisive culture within a team. After hearing these negative comments over and over again, the athlete will eventually believe it. Over time, this will lead to negative attitude and effort, ultimately resulting in a selfish teammate.

Now, let's put yourself in the scenario where your child comes home after a game in which he or she did not play. What do you say?

The first thing you could do is talk about the game itself. Recount certain plays and make note of individuals who played well for both teams. This initial conversation removes the uncomfortable nature of the situation and sets the stage to discuss how your child feels about not getting into the game. Sometimes your child may be upset, angry, or even embarrassed and will not want to talk about it. These moments of silence give parents an opportunity to explain the importance of being a good teammate--how all members of the team can have a major impact, no matter what role they play. These moments can help illustrate the value of being the first person off the bench to congratulate or offer words of encouragement.

Parents can also talk about how the harder one works in practice, the better the team is going to be. In other words, we have the responsibility as parents to teach our kids the significance of living life "pointed out," regardless of their circumstances. Living "pointed out" simply means to put others before yourself in everything you do. It is finding ways to make those around you the best they can be. No complaining. No excuses.

Andrew DeWitt participated in two years of varsity basketball for me at Hudsonville but he rarely had the opportunity to play. Unfortunately for him, he was a good player on two really good teams, both boasting a ton of talent. He understood his role and treated every practice like a game, always playing as hard as he could. Every day, he would elevate the intensity of practice. On game nights, he was our biggest cheerleader. His impact transcended scoring points and getting rebounds. Andrew's parents, when it would have been easy for them to make excuses or complain, were effective teachers as they guided him through those tough times. They taught Andrew that, no matter what role you play, you can always have an influence on other people's lives. What a great lesson Andrew can carry with him for the rest of his life.

At the end of the day, one thing every parent in every situation can say that will have a positive impact is "I love you." Often, student-athletes think they are letting their parents down because of their lack of playing time. Therefore, it is vitally important for student-athletes to know that their parents love them the same, whether they play a lot or not at all. This will have a significant impact on how he or she learns to respond to adversity.

I challenge all parents to use these potentially negative situations as opportunities to teach their student-athletes valuable lessons on what it means to be a great teammate; more importantly, use them to illustrate the value of living their lives "pointed out." You may not have a handy six-word phrase that helps when your child does not play, but you definitely have plenty to talk about.

Inside the Huddle
How have you responded when your child struggles to perform well or does not play?

Executing the Play

Avoid negative conversations in the car on the drive home from a contest. As a parent, if you are upset with your child's performance or playing time, establish for yourself a minimum amount of time before you talk about it. See if he or she comes to you first.

30 Second Timeout

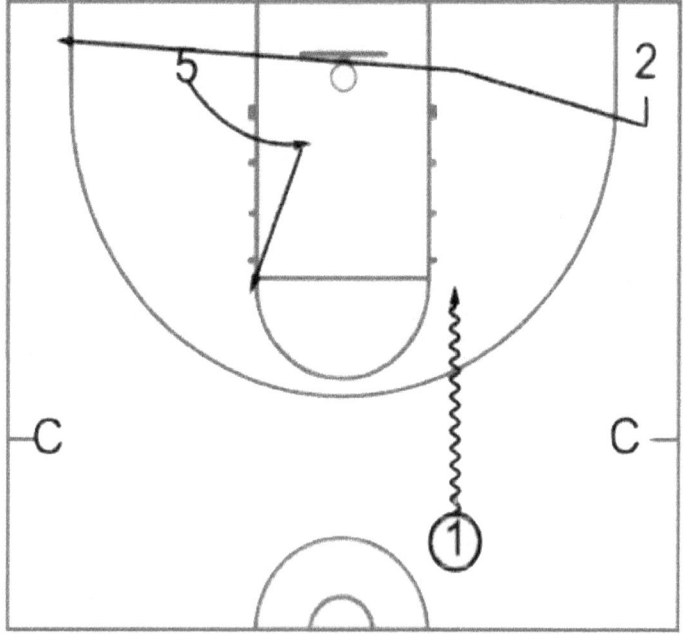

THE GAME OUTSIDE OF THE GAME

My heart was pounding, my hands were sweating, and I found myself wanting to pace. However, I knew my pacing would probably make my son more nervous than he already was. He had just lost three games of tennis in a row, shrinking his set score to 5-4. He did end up winning the next game which ended the match. *Whew!* I could breathe again!

Why as parents do we get so caught up in our child's performance? For some parents, it is because of the time and money spent on the sport. They are looking for a return on their investment. Other parents view their child's success as a way to increase their social status. For me and many other parents, watching our kids struggle and fail is difficult because we love them and want the best for them. I once heard a golf parent say, as he watched his daughter score 10 on her first hole, "This is the most difficult thing I have ever endured." This parent later explained that he could neither fix his daughter's problem nor console her. This proves how powerful the emotion of sports can be.

What we may not realize is how strongly our actions directly influence the performance of our children. Our kids are extremely perceptive and can be affected by our verbal cues as well as body language. Last fall I witnessed an example of this at the MHSAA Golf State Finals. I observed a player hit an errant iron shot, only to then look and see her dad raise his arms in disbelief. The same girl then missed an easy putt and when she looked back, she watched her dad put his head down in his hands. On the next hole, after another errant shot, her dad walked away in disgust. The player continued to struggle, hole after hole, because her dad's body language was a greater concern for her than focusing on her game.

Another example of a parent's body language impacting a contest happened at a basketball game while I was an athletic director. A dad was found visibly pacing back and forth behind the bench as the game approached its final minutes. The more he paced, the more the team panicked down the stretch. His nervous energy was mirrored by the girls on the court. The girls continued to make mistakes and hurried their shots. The team's lack of poise ultimately led to their defeat.

Here are a few ways we can control our emotions and body language while watching our student-athletes play:

1. Proximity. Where you sit or watch a contest can have a significant influence on your body language. The farther you are from the competition, the easier it becomes to control your body language and the less your child will notice you.

2. Stand or sit? For some sports, spectators are required to sit while other sports allow them to move more freely. If you are standing, be sure to avoid pacing because that can become destructive. Your child will sense this and you will see their anxiousness increase as your pacing increases.

3. With whom to sit? If you are sitting with negative people, the more likely you are to become negative. This negativity will be on full display for everyone--including your child--to see. Let the negative people sit alone.

4. Watch the team. We get so caught up with watching our own kids, it is easy to forget that the success of any team is achieved by more than one player. If your child is involved in a team sport, spend more time watching the ball and less time watching only him or her. In individual sports (like tennis, golf, and cross country), take time to watch all the players compete. Watching other athletes can bring your focus more on the team and less on the individual. This will also bring your stress level down because you can use your nervous energy to cheer on others, rather than worrying only about your child.

Nobody ever said being a parent of an athlete is easy. Remember how much of a privilege it is to watch our sons and daughters compete on the athletic field. Time passes too quickly. Before we know it, this opportunity to watch our kids will be over. Let's all take a 30 second timeout to adopt new, fresh, positive attitudes as we watch our children participate in the sports they love.

Inside the Huddle
As a parent, what do you struggle with the most while watching your child participate in sports?

Executing the Play
The more vocally negative people are in the stands, the farther away you want to be. Misery loves company. Make those people the minority, not the majority.

30 Second Timeout

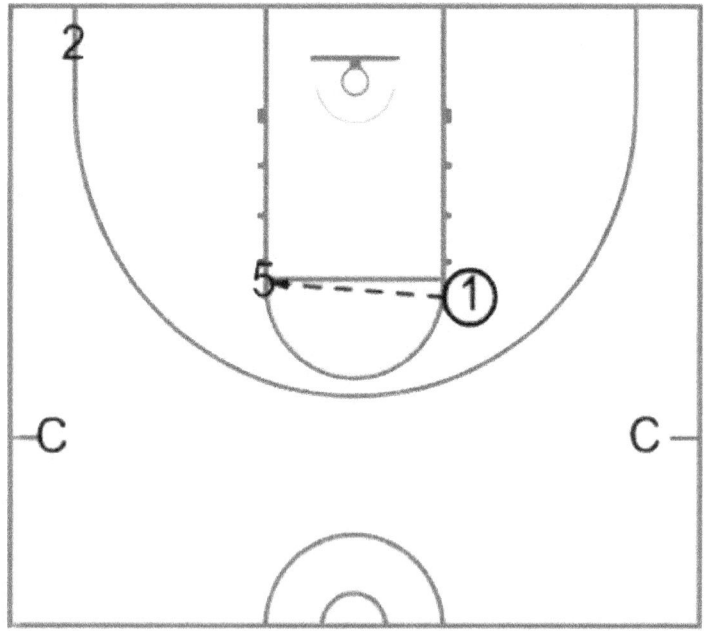

ARE YOU INVOLVED OR COMMITTED?

One of my favorite principles from Tim Elmore's *Habitudes: The Art of Self-Leadership* is called the "Half-Hearted Mountain Climber." Dr. Elmore tells the story of a group of mountain climbers who begin their ascent to the top of the Swiss Alps. Roughly halfway up they reach a warming house where they rest their legs and take in a bite to eat. After about an hour, half of the group decides to stop and remain in the comfortable lodge. The other half continues on to the summit.

Those climbers who reach the top of the Swiss Alps not only enjoy the greatest view they have ever seen, but they also are awarded the satisfaction of completing an arduous journey that challenged both their minds and bodies. The individuals who made it halfway were *involved* while those who made it to the top were *committed*. In an expedition like this, people who are merely involved will stop when things get difficult. Committed individuals, however, will readily fight through challenges to reach their goals. This simple story can have a profound impact on the way student-athletes and their parents live their lives.

How do we know if we are involved or committed?

Let's look at the student-athlete first. Involved student-athletes are those who do not work very hard to better themselves as students or athletes. They are concerned more with individual awards than team accomplishments. They will often complain about their playing time, the coach, or teammates. These are the same students who say they love the sport, but yet will make unhealthy choices when it comes to alcohol, drugs, and social media use.

What do you think committed student-athletes look like? They are those who understand that being a "student-athlete" means one must be a student first. They treat their classmates and teachers with respect. Committed student-athletes will never complain about playing time and will accept whatever role they are assigned; they know that if they do their best, it will ultimately help the team become its best. Commitment means making good decisions when it comes to alcohol, drugs, and social media. Partaking in alcohol and drugs or using social media in harmful or inappropriate ways not only violates the handbook they signed, it also shows that they consider themselves more important than the team.

In the end, it is easier to be involved because being committed means that everything one does must contribute to the betterment of both team and school. This will require sacrifice and hard work. A committed athlete, very simply, does it the "right way." I have seen so many teams compete over my years as a coach and athletic director. The great teams all seem to possess one common element: They all have very committed student-athletes. As an athlete, are you committed?

How does this principle apply to parents of student-athletes? Involved parents are the first to call the coach when their son or daughter is not getting the playing time they think is deserved. Involved parents are those who loudly criticize officials at games and who coach from the sideline, placing immense pressure on their child to perform well. An involved parent is more concerned about a college athletic scholarship than an academic scholarship.

What are the essential qualities of committed parents? These parents understand that athletics offer their kids experiences that hold the potential to transform their lives. They acknowledge the fact that there will be adverse situations their children will have to navigate and work through without them. Committed parents encourage their son or daughter to deal with playing time issues by initiating a conversation with the coach. These parents cheer for every player on the team and they are willing to support the program in any way possible. As a parent, it is easy to be involved, but very challenging to be committed--it requires a conscious effort to see the "big picture." That being said, committed parents help shape committed kids, and this will lead to committed programs. As a parent, are you committed?

Another way to understand Dr. Elmore's principle is by taking a look at a ham and egg breakfast. The chicken was involved but the pig was committed. As we know, every season presents many challenges along with many celebrations. We have two choices in regard to how the season will go: Are we going to be the chicken (involved) or are we going to be the pig (committed)?

Inside the Huddle
How committed are you as a parent? What are some things you do well and what are some areas in which you would like to improve?

Executing the Play
Work together with your child to brainstorm a list of positive habits he or she can practice to become more committed as a student-athlete?

30 Second Timeout

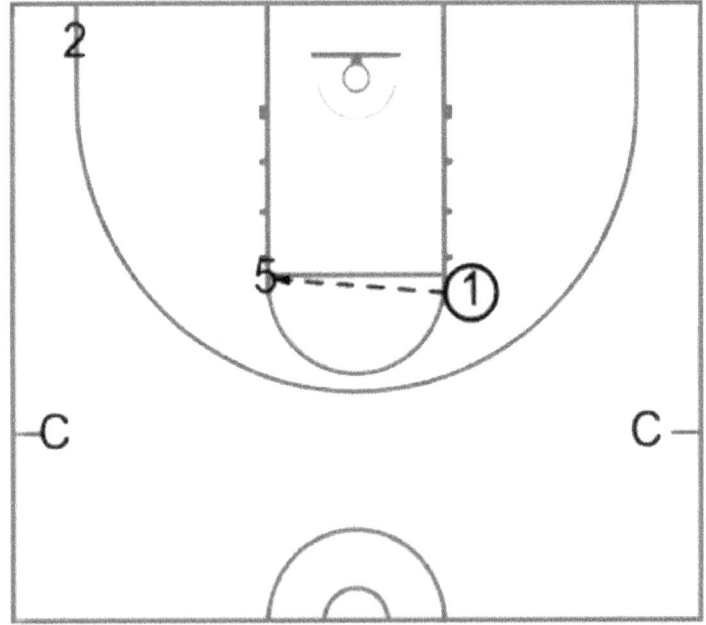

ONE WORD

How can one word change our lives when, on average, people speak between 7,000 to 20,000 words per day? Jon Gordon, Dan Britton, and Jimmy Page wrote a book together about this very subject: How one word can impact our lives at home, work, church, or wherever we want that focus to be.

I was a little hesitant to read the book because of its simplicity, but because Jon Gordon is my favorite author, I thought I would give it a try. My initial skepticism was replaced with the realization that this did, in fact, make a lot of sense. Reading their stories and considering the process left me intrigued and questioning how I could use this concept at work and at home.

The basis of the principle is that people have a hard time focusing on long-winded mission statements or New Year's resolutions because they are composed of too many words that are often forgotten. According to a study by the University of Scranton, only eight percent of people who make New Year's resolutions are successful in achieving their goals. However, one word sticks.

We have instituted this One Word concept at our high school by having teachers choose one word that will make an impact in their classrooms. This has inspired a trickle-down effect as some teachers have asked their students to choose one word that will impact their own lives. Some of our students even had their one word shown on *The*

Today Show as a part of an interview with Jon Gordon on New Year's Day!

According to *One Word That Will Change Your Life*, discovering your one word can be achieved by doing the following: First, you need to prepare your heart by unplugging all the noise around you, regardless of what is producing it. This noise could come from one of the following or a combination of them: your cell phone, TV, the computer, a busy schedule, etc. Then you answer the following questions:

- What are my needs?
- What is in my way of achieving my needs?
- What needs to go in order to move forward?

Once you have your one word, you need to live it out. If your word is going to stick, you must find places to post it so that you have daily reminders. Some people will post the word on their refrigerator, bathroom mirror, screen saver on their computer, or even set it as a reminder on their phone. Have fun with this part because the more you make your word a part of your life, the more of an impact it is going to have.

"Experience" was one of the words I have chosen in the past. As our kids are getting older, my wife and I are realizing that they will soon be out of the house. We do not want every memory of childhood focused on travel baseball and tennis tournaments. We want our kids to experience more than just sports. How often have you gotten away from town, headed to the beach, gone on a vacation, or simply stayed home playing cards with your kids? Those experiences will create memories that will last a lifetime. This past Christmas our kids reminded us how important these experiences are when they presented us with a 24 x 30" canvas photograph of them in a rowboat on a glacier lake in Alaska, the Alaskan mountain range towering behind them.

Of all the things they could have given us for Christmas, this meant the most to them. This was their way of thanking us for all the adventures we have gone on together. The word "experience" has made a tremendous impact on our family. More than I would've ever imagined.

What word could you choose for your son or daughter's next season? Youth sports can bring out just about every emotion possible, often causing us to feel like we are on a constant roller coaster. There will be highs, lows, frustrations, doubts, celebrations, and everything in between. I would find that my own mood was just a reflection of my children's performance on the playing field. A few years ago when my son was younger, he struck out three times in one game and it affected the rest of the weekend. On the flip side, when my son won a tennis match for which he was a significant underdog, I was extremely happy the rest of the night.

We react this way as parents because we love our kids and want the best for them all the time. Having one word, however, can put the focus on something other than just the success and failure they will encounter. It will help juggle the emotions that go into watching our kids perform. I encourage all parents to find their word and live it every day--it will only help as we steer ourselves through the challenges of youth sports.

Inside the Huddle
Have everyone in your family choose one word, for either the upcoming season or for the entire year.

Executing the Play
Hold your family accountable for their one word by displaying everyone's word on a single piece of paper. Or, set it as a reminder on each of their cell phones where everyone will see it every day.

30 Second Timeout

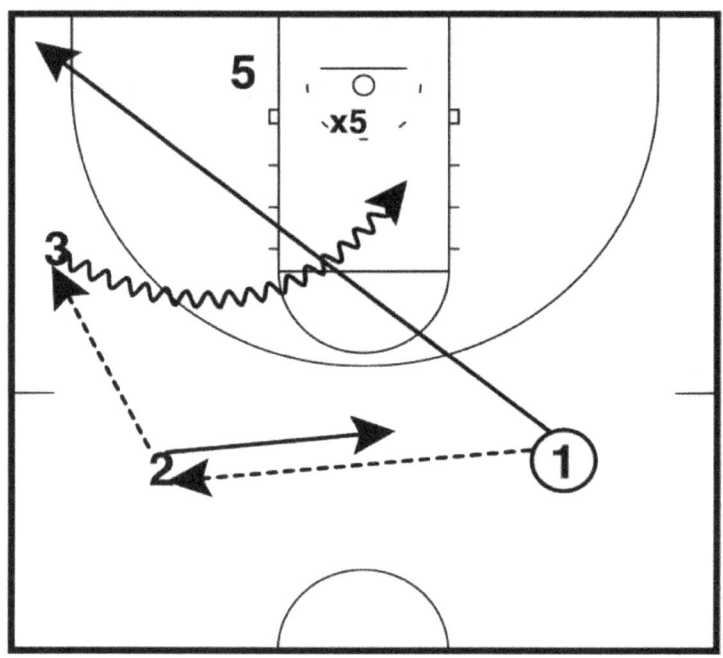

PARTNERSHIP

One word that can further enhance your team, program, or school is "partnership."

Often, roadblocks are established within athletic programs, preventing them from reaching their fullest potential. This creates an internal separation, one where all involved partners detach themselves from the values and goals set by the institution. We can find this in virtually every organization, but this chapter is going to specifically focus on the partnerships among parents, coaches, student-athletes, and officials.

During my basketball coaching career, I encountered a set of parents who were unhappy about what they considered a reduced role for their child on the team. He was a starter his sophomore and junior year, but the dynamics of the team his senior year had shifted; they required that I move him because he was one of my best offensive players and he could help the second unit. He would play about the same number of minutes, but his role would have to change.

As a coaching staff, we believed this change helped the team, but it also helped the student-athlete by allowing him to use his strengths as an offensive player. He would have more opportunities to score than if he had remained a starter. We were trying to do what was best for both the team and individual, but the parents did not see it that way. Attempts to reason with them only made the situation worse because they felt he was entitled to start. They did not appreciate the fact that we were offering him a greater opportunity to reach his fullest potential.

The parents went to the extreme of distributing a petition for my removal as head coach; they also told anyone who would listen how bad of a coach I was. This type of partnership caused dissension within our team. While his parents created a negative atmosphere in the stands, the player complained openly to his teammates, creating a negative atmosphere in our locker room. Needless to say, that was a tough season to build a cohesive group.

This story provides insight on how one isolated incident can have an impact on so many other partnerships. The parent-coach partnership was strained along with the player-coach partnership. The negative culture that grew within this situation inhibited the growth of the team and its ability to reach its potential. The parent-child partnership was also directly affected because the parents assumed the role of agent or defender, not one of supporter or advisor. Just think if the parents had talked to their child and said, "This is a great opportunity for you and your team. You could see a lot of benefit by supplying the scoring load off the bench. If this makes the team better, you should embrace it." Had they handled the circumstances differently, the season and its outcome could have had an entirely different feel.

Every season will bring with it some adversity and "why" moments, but having an open and positive communication line with the coach and your child is the key to forming positive partnerships. You don't have to always agree with the decisions, but how you handle those "why" moments will have a profound impact on both your child and the team.

One type of partnership I did not describe in that story, but is becoming more and more fractured every year, is the parent-fan-official partnership. Once a group of officials asked me to sit in the stands of an opposing team because of how degrading the spectators were toward the officials. On more than one occasion, I have had to talk to a group of fans and ask them to keep it positive. Most of the time they've looked at me as if to reply, "You can't tell me what I can and can't say." What many people fail to understand is that yelling at an official has no bearing on the game. An official has never changed a call based on a fan's reaction to it. For two straight years we have seen a steady decline of officials. While many leave the profession, very few people are entering it. Do you blame them? Who wants to work two or three days per week only to get yelled at for hours at a time.

My challenge to you is to be different. Do not conform with what is going on in gyms and fields all over America. Be different. Choose to enhance those partnerships that allow for healthy, strong athletic programs. One way to do this is by giving our officials an applause when introduced for every contest. After the game, thank them for their time and efforts. I encourage anyone out there who has an interest in officiating to give it a try. It is another way you can have a powerful impact on student-athletes.

Partnership is one critical component necessary in the building of a positive and sustainable culture. Think of a way in which you can strengthen a partnership within your child's athletic experience. It will surely make a difference.

Inside the Huddle
Why can it be challenging to cultivate partnerships in youth sports?

Executing the Play
Ask your coach for ways you can help during the course of the season. Maybe it is organizing a food schedule or maybe it is taking stats or filming games. If you look, you will find many ways to support your son or daughter's team.

30 Second Timeout

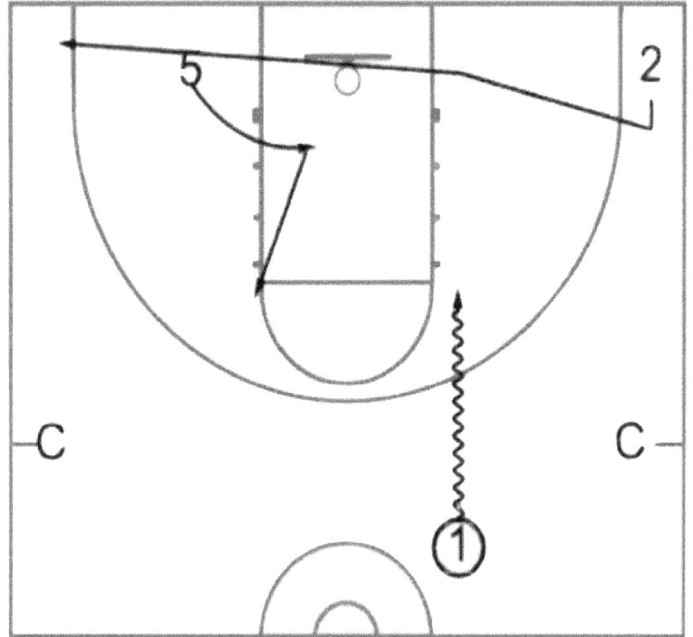

MOTIVATION

While watching your child compete, how often have you thought, *Why doesn't he play hard?* or *Why doesn't she seem motivated?* Motivating our sons and daughters in any area of life is one of the most challenging things we face as parents. Addressing this issue and being able to answer those questions may have a tremendous impact on the growth and development of our children, no matter their age.

As parents, the first question we need to ask is, "Whose goal is it?" The goals or expectations we have for our kids too often meet our own selfish needs rather than the needs of the particular child. Our dreams may not be their dreams.

I once had a conversation with a college coach about this very subject. He so badly wanted his daughter to play volleyball, compete at a high level, and someday play in college. His daughter listened to him and did everything he said. She played travel volleyball along with high school volleyball and developed into a really good player. Her dad noticed, however, that she was never very excited about all of her accomplishments and wondered why she did not seem very motivated. One day his daughter revealed to him that she wanted to stop playing and just focus on becoming an artist. *Artist*???

He could not believe his daughter would rather study art than play volleyball. She reluctantly went on to play college volleyball for a couple of years until finally deciding she had lost the will to compete. Again, she explained to her dad that all she wanted to do was become an artist.

Her dad, disappointed and confused, worried that this choice would have very little influence in her life, that it would not prepare her for the world that lay ahead. The exact opposite happened: She graduated with honors and received her doctorate. She now owns an art studio on the East Coast and runs an art school. Why did she have so much success? Because despite her dad's dreams for her, she'd found her own passion.

One of the primary elements of motivation for our children is for them to discover their passions. Naturally, we are all more motivated when we love what we are doing. That is the easy part of motivation. The real question becomes, "How do we motivate our sons or daughters when something is *not* their natural passion?" By definition, motivation is the process which guides and maintains goal-oriented behaviors. According to Greg Shelley in his article, "5 Keys to Motivating your Athletes," motivation can come in different forms.

Some people use fear tactics to motivate. Threatening children and using consequences may seem like it works in the short term. However, when practiced consistently, they will lose their passion and the sport is no longer fun. Many athletes have quit their favorite sport because of this.

Incentives are also only short term means to motivate. Over time, athletes will lose the desire to play because the incentive begins to overshadow the reason they began playing the sport in the first place. In order to create any long term motivation, student-athletes need to understand the purpose of "*Why* am I involved with this sport?" This understanding helps create an environment of personal growth in which athletes are encouraged to motivate themselves.

To assist our children in recognizing their own purpose, we can simply ask them what it is they want out of the experience and why they participate in the sports they choose. This simple exercise will prove essential for parents in determining whether or not their children's goals are different from their own.

As parents, it is easy for us to be more concerned with the outcome rather than the process. For instance, my two daughters play sports for completely different reasons. My oldest daughter loves to practice and compete, while my youngest loves to be a part of a team. In short, I motivate my oldest daughter differently than my youngest based on what each wants out of the experience. After identifying our children's personal goals, we can use that information to more effectively motivate them to reach their full potential.

Another way parents can assist in motivating their sons and daughters, especially during periods of struggle, is to have them recall a time when they had experienced success in that particular sport. As a coach, I tried this motivational technique with one of my golf teams on the way to a match. Because we had lost our two previous matches, I asked each golfer to talk about a great shot she had hit during the course of the year. After doing this for ten minutes, I told them that if they start to struggle, they need to think about all the great shots they had hit that season. Not only did each player shoot a season low, but the team broke the school record that day! The power of positive thinking is always a great motivational tool.

As we know, motivation can be a complex subject, but my hope is that these tools will be useful as you are navigating this journey. Identifying goals and focusing on the positive will allow our kids to develop long-term motivation that will last well after the game is over. Remember, our goals may not be their goals.

Inside the Huddle
What are some of the barriers that get in the way of our children giving their best possible effort?

Executing the Play
In every conversation you have with your child in regard to performance, make sure you are talking about the process and not the outcome. Identify those things that are integral parts of the process.

30 Second Timeout

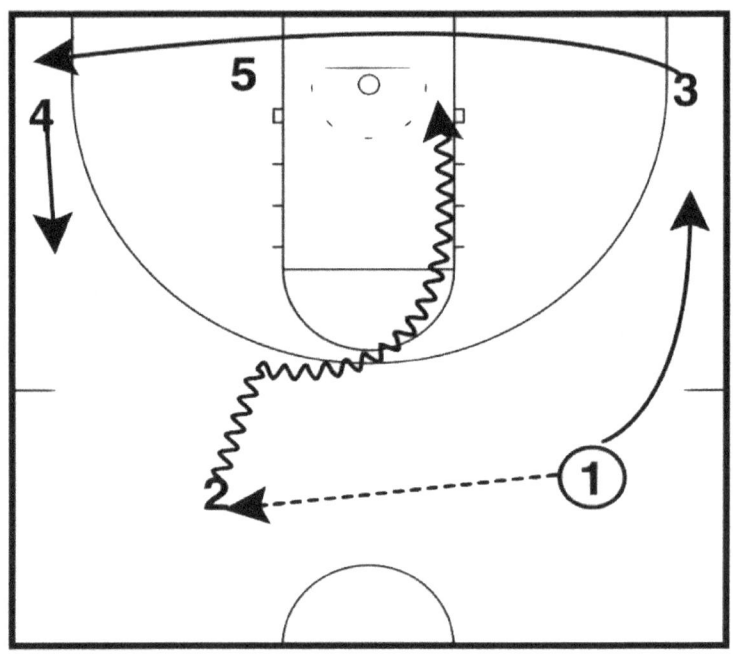

PERSPECTIVE

Bases are loaded with two outs in the last inning. If we score one more run, our team advances to the championship game. My son is up to bat. Having played a great game to this point, the stage is set for him to get a walk-off base-hit and have the team mob him after crossing first base. Although two quick strikes put him in a hole, he battles back to a full count. But he then swings weakly at a high pitch and pops it up to the second baseman. Game over. As he walks back to the dugout, I can see the disappointment on his face because, in his mind, that single at-bat cost his team a chance to play for the championship. As parents, it is difficult to see our children go through adversity and, in those moments, we wish for "do-overs" so the outcomes can be different.

It is two weeks later on the morning of July 2. My wife and I wake up and decide to go for a walk while on vacation in Saginaw Bay. Not more than a 100 meters into the walk, my left calf begins to spasm. Immediately, I know the blood clots are back. Over the years, I have had multiple bypass surgeries and other procedures to eliminate blood clots in the same calf. *How can this happen again?* On our drive back to Grand Rapids to see my vascular surgeon, many "Why me?" thoughts cross my mind, but knowing that I have dealt with this adversity before provides some comfort. For as much of a nuisance these blood clots have become, I know I will be OK.

July 4. At the hospital I am able to leave my floor and spend time with two of the most inspirational people I know. Spencer Meyer is a seven-year-old who has been battling leukemia for years, and Thomas Sikkema is a high school senior who was recently diagnosed with a brain tumor. I am continuously amazed at how their families fight through the most adverse conditions with such tremendous positivity. My blood clots will soon be gone, but these young men will continue to battle cancer and the effects of treatment. All of us can draw strength from these families when we have to deal with our own personal problems. They can help us keep things in perspective.

Perspective.

Looking back, I am glad my son popped out to end the game. For the rest of his life, he will be able to draw on that experience as he encounters the setbacks awaiting him in the future. Of course, there will also be those moments in life when he gets the "big hit." No matter where you are in this odyssey, make sure you keep in perspective what high school and youth sports should be all about. Our children will experience both success and struggle throughout their athletic careers, and the mission of youth sports is to employ both in the process of transforming their lives for the better. Please remember the "Youth Sports Parent Athletic Creed" as we strive to provide the best experience for our student-athletes:

- **Parents will understand their role.**
- **Parents will equally support and encourage their child and his/her teammates and coaches, no matter the outcome.**
- **Parents will act with the highest class possible in all situations.**
- **Parents will allow their children to face adversity.**

Inside the Huddle
What are the moments in your life or your child's life that have brought about a sense of perspective?

Executing the Play
The next time your children face adversity in athletics, show them how to handle it with support, dignity, and class. By doing this, you are modeling how they can positively react when they someday become parents themselves.

OFFICIALS

We were five seconds away from one of the greatest upsets in the history of Caledonia basketball.

During the regular season, South Christian High School had beaten us by more than thirty points on two different occasions. On a warm March day, the district finals became the site for the third and final contest between us. We were able to slow them down just enough to stay within striking distance until late in the fourth quarter when we finally took the lead for the first time. South Christian had one last chance with seven seconds left on the clock. After a timeout, they inbounded the ball from the sideline and their player forced up a shot. From my viewpoint, I could see it was going to be short and my heart began to race with adrenaline as I sensed that the impossible was going to become possible. But what happened next would stick with me for years: One of the South Christian players pushed one of our players in the back, grabbed the rebound, and put the ball in the basket with one second left. Game over. South Christian had won the district championship.

Over the course of my coaching career I still held a grudge against officials for that one call. Twelve years later and no longer coaching, I went back and re-watched the game for the first time. I almost turned off the video before the last seven seconds because I did not want to relive that moment and the ensuing emotions that took place. While watching, however, I discovered something: The South Christian player did not shove my player as much as I had thought, and our players did not box out as well as I had thought, which made it easier for them to get the rebound and score. Thinking back to that last timeout before the ball was inbounded, did I even tell my players to box out?

At that moment it became very clear to me that what we see during a game may be clouded because we want our team to gain every advantage in order to be successful. Perception is not always reality.

Officials are human. They make mistakes just as coaches and players do during a game. There has never been a game solely decided by an official. Some people claim that the Class B semifinal boys basketball game was decided by one call. The officials had ruled that the foot of a Forest Hills Northern player was on the line on his last second shot, while in fact video would show later, his foot clearly was behind it. That call seemed to cost them a chance to play in the state finals. Coach Steve Harvey handled the situation with a tremendous amount of class. He was quoted in the paper saying, "We had our chances at the end, it did not have to come down to that last shot," Harvey said. "We could and should have taken care of it earlier. We just did not play our typical game, for whatever reason, we did not take the charges, we did not play the tough defense we have all year." At the moment, it seemed like that one call cost Forest Hills Northern the contest. However, over fifty offensive and defensive possessions preceded that play, and all of them contributed to the game's eventual outcome.

Having the opportunity to spend time with officials inside the locker room has made it very evident to me that they are serious about their jobs and want nothing but to call the best game possible. Some, an hour and a half before their contest begins, have requested a monitor to break down film; they want to identify strengths and weaknesses in their placement and mechanics from prior contests. I have witnessed officials upset at halftime or after a game because they realized they had made a mistake. Officials have later personally contacted me to apologize for a call made during a game.

In the business world as well as in education, we often use the word "collaboration." In athletics, officials collaborate before, during, and after every contest to garner more knowledge so they can continue to improve. For most officials this is not even their full-time job. Officials do what they do because they love the game and want to give back to the sport that made an impact on them. The next time we are at a game and we think the officials missed a call, let's take a 30 second timeout to gather our emotions so that we do not say anything we will later regret. Let's simply spend our energy cheering on our teams to be the best they can be.

Inside the Huddle
How often have you seen an official overturn a call because it was challenged by a spectator? Why do spectators in the stands yell at officials?

Executing the Play
Cheer for the officials as they are introduced at the beginning of each game. Any time you get the chance, thank an official for his or her service.

30 Second Timeout

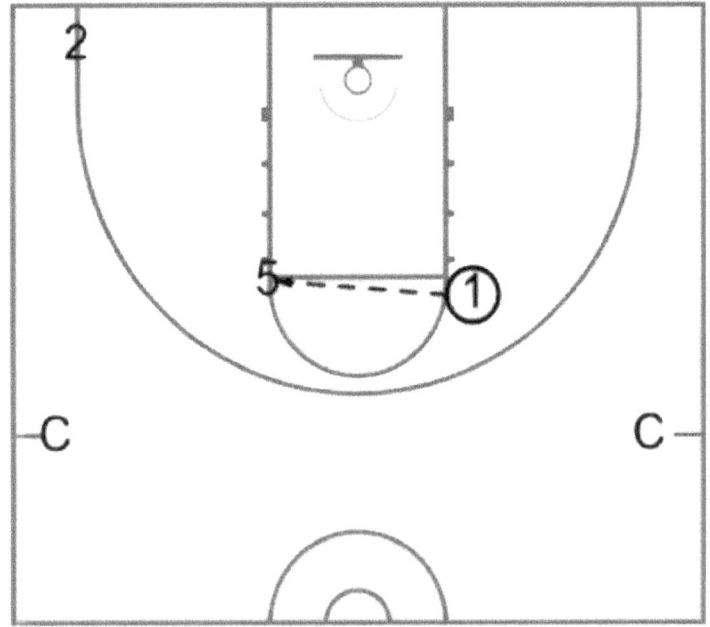

RELEASE

"Release the club" is common terminology when teaching the golf swing. A tight end in football may "release" on a play and become a receiver. In basketball, a player may be "released" to start a fast break. As coaches, we motivate our athletes to "release" their adrenaline and encourage them to "release" their inner drive.

As parents of student-athletes, does "release" hold any relevance?

Absolutely.

One of the single most important things we can do for our children is to "release" them to the game. This means that when they become part of a team, our role is to take a back seat and be their biggest fans, not to become interventionists when things do not go well. Why is this so difficult for many parents? The answer to this question involves two entities: control and money. With kids participating in sports at such an early age, their first coach is often their actual parent. As children grow and progress, they will have different coaches who have their own philosophies. Because these philosophies may be different and concepts not taught the same way, the parent-coach has a hard time releasing his or her child to the game.

I have experienced this as both a parent and a coach. I distinctly remember, during my first year as a varsity basketball coach, having a conversation with a parent who turned it into a philosophical debate. He made it a point to tell me, over and over, that thirty years ago he had played on the last conference championship team. He tried to reason that they had won because they played a zone defense, and that our current team could never win playing man-to-man. Well, we won games and lost games during my tenure as a Varsity basketball coach, but neither had anything to do with the type of defense we played.

Duke and Syracuse are consistently two of the best college basketball programs in the country. When Coach K started at Duke, his teams would never play a second of zone defense, while Syracuse would never play a second of man-to-man. The game can be taught in such a wide variety of ways. I have been a coach for more than half of my life. I am also a parent. Those two roles can sometimes be one and the same but when they are not, and I drop off my kids at practice, I know that I need to go home. If I stay, I will be tempted to critique, which would be unfair to both my kids and their coach.

Money is another factor that can deter parents from releasing their child to the game. AAU and other travel sports organizations are large businesses that allow players more opportunities to gain experience and improve individual skills. They also can be very expensive. Because their roles and expectations may differ from those of the school's program, their cost may create difficulty for parents to "release" their child to the school team.

For example, one AAU volleyball organization may have three middle hitters who all enjoy a great deal of playing time. When they try out for the school's volleyball team, however, only one will get the starting job, requiring the other two girls to take on completely different roles. This experience allows these two girls an opportunity to learn something about themselves and how to deal with these types of situations. That is, if their parents resist becoming interventionists and are willing to "release" them to the game. Spending money on travel sports does not entitle anyone to anything.

The problem with an unwillingness to release one's child to the game centers around another word: trust. When parents do not trust the coach and they communicate this distrust to their child, it sends a mixed message. The message at home will leave doubt within the athlete, who then will not buy into the program. Ultimately, the athlete's production and the team's performance will suffer, all because the parents would not "release" their son or daughter to the game.

Being a parent of an athlete presents many challenges. We all want the best for our kids, and when things don't go as planned, we want to solve the problem for them. Instead, we need to be empathetic listeners, helping our kids face the realities of adversity in positive ways. No season is going to be perfect and not every coach is going to be a favorite. Looking back, my least favorite seasons as an athlete in high school were those that shaped me the most into the person I am today. My hope is that the word "release" will allow you to enjoy the process, because these moments of youth sports will not last forever.

Inside the Huddle
On a scale of 1-10, where do you rate yourself when it comes to releasing your child to the game? What reasons do you have for that rating?

Executing the Play
The next time a problem arises, instead of trying to solve it yourself, ask your child how he or she thinks the situation should be handled.

30 Second Timeout

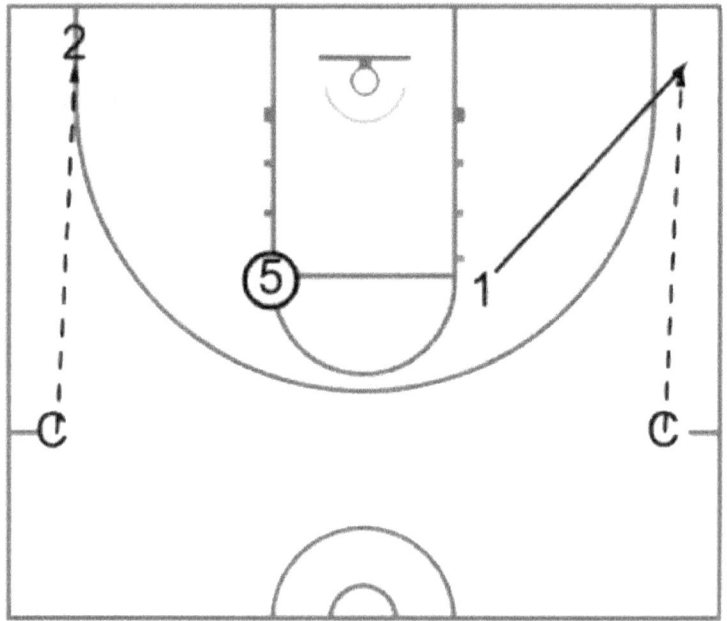

CHOICES

Choices.

Every day provides us many opportunities to make them. Sometimes our choices are wise and sometimes they are regrettable. High school athletes are also presented with many choices. Some of those include:

- What type of effort will we put forth into the particular sport we play?
- What type of attitude will we display when things are not going well?
- How will we treat our teammates and coaches?
- What decisions will we make off the field regarding drugs and alcohol?

The use of drugs and alcohol--and now electronic cigarettes and vaping devices--remains a battle we face at the middle and high school levels within our athletic programs. We all have policies in place to deter this behavior, yet it continues. Improper decisions not only take away from individual performance, but they also hurt the team no matter what role the athlete plays. Kirk Cousins said it best during a speech at Michigan State when he talked about how athletes are privileged, and with that privilege comes great responsibility. That responsibility is not just during the season, but it is important 365 days a year. The responsibility to make good decisions requires discipline, and discipline is another wonderful quality that sports can teach our kids.

How can parents reading this spread the message and create healthy "safe havens" for their student-athletes when they want to hang out together?

Parents should talk with their children and devise a plan of action to follow in case drugs or alcohol ever become present while they are at somebody else's house. We want our students to be comfortable knowing that they can call someone if they need to be picked up. For any athletes reading this, you have the opportunity to impact the culture within your school district by exemplifying this message: Being involved in drugs and alcohol is not the right thing to do.

It takes a collaborative effort to keep our students safe and help them make the best choices possible.

Most students today are also forced to make choices regarding social media. High school students will spend anywhere from one to nine hours per day in front of a screen. Most of the screen time is used to connect with people through apps like Snapchat and Instagram. This generation of students was born into a culture of technology, and technology will continue to be an integral part of their lives. When I first bought an iPhone, my kids helped me figure out how to use it. The crazy part is that none of them owned a cell phone at the time!

I attended a conference led by Dr. Tim Elmore who said something that still resonates with me: "Students today are more connected but less involved." Our students are connected through so many different social media outlets, yet they are less likely to communicate face to face or even over the phone. And therein lies the danger.

Every generation preceding what Dr. Elmore dubs this current "iY Generation" has lived a "closed life," one in which people communicated one on one, in person or over the phone. It was the complete opposite of the very "open life" being lived by this generation. From tweets to posts on Snapchat, Instagram, and even Facebook, anyone can find out what someone else is doing or feeling at any time of the day or night. And, technology is not going away.

As parents, how can we educate kids to use technology effectively as well as positively? The answer to this question centers around the word "awareness." It sure seems simple enough, but because technology changes constantly, it becomes difficult for parents to keep up with the latest social media outlets. This may take a little work on our part as parents, but just Googling the different social media will, at the very least, give us an understanding of how they work. If nothing else, realizing the complexity and power of technology will create an awareness of what your children could be doing on their electronic devices. Do you know what apps they have? Are they on Instagram? TikTok? Snapchat? Twitter?

Hopefully, this chapter will encourage a conversation between you and your children regarding what they are using and how they are using it. Once you have identified the apps and social media they are using, the next step is to monitor them. Because each child needs to learn how to use social media appropriately, this does not mean you have to "hover" over everything they post. Asking questions about why they posted a certain picture on Instagram or what a particular tweet means can go a long way in teaching students how to use social media both effectively and appropriately. Again, technology is not going away, so parents must play a lead role in teaching their children how to use it.

The bottom line is that if we do not educate our kids on this issue, who will? One of the leading reasons so many in this generation misuse social media is that no one has taught them how to use it. It seems that whenever I have a conversation with student-athletes because of their misuse of social media, it always comes back to an ignorance of the potential implications, which consistently stems from the lack of education. They do not realize that although a Snapchat picture only lasts six seconds, anyone can screenshot it and save it to share, even in the distant future. The same goes with deleted tweets or Facebook posts. That is why, given our own lack of knowledge, at least being aware can go a long way in holding our kids accountable and educating them on how to use their electronics.

Our student-athletes are forced to navigate countless choices each and every day. The most challenging part of being a parent may be helping our kids learn to maneuver through them. If we want our children to be successful both in and out of sports, we must take the initiative to play a more integral role in guiding them toward prudent and positive decision-making. Before they move on toward their next destinations in life, we must travel beside them now, making their journeys as valuable as possible.

Inside the Huddle
Have a conversation with your children to discuss all the social media apps they use throughout the course of a day.

Executing the Play
Devise a plan to hold your children accountable for their social media use. Could you set limits on their screen time? Could you monitor their usage by inspecting their phones?

BIG MIKE CHALLENGE

What is your favorite athletic moment?

As years pass, some people may look back at one of our conference, district, regional, or state championships as a special moment they will never forget. Maybe an indelible memory was born from an extraordinary team performance in a regular season game or even from an amazing individual accomplishment. The list may be long but at the end of the day, we can all be proud of our student-athletes by how they've represented themselves both in and out of competition.

For me, the highlight of the 2013-14 athletic season did not happen during the heat of competition, and it did not involve one of our "athletes." My highlight occurred on May 21 in the high school cafeteria.

This was our Senior Athletic Awards Ceremony, an opportunity for our Athletic Department to offer one last "Thank you" and "Congratulations" to the outgoing seniors for their accomplishments and dedication to Hudsonville Athletics. On this particular night, we were able to recognize one student whose impact on our athletic teams extended far beyond anything we could measure or even begin to describe. This moment belonged to Michael Kempema or "Big Mike" as we all affectionately call him.

Because of developmental disorders, Big Mike never played an inning of baseball or a minute of basketball, but that never stopped him from making a difference. Dave VanNoord, Hudsonville's varsity baseball coach, said this when I asked him about Mike:

> "Michael Kempema has been a special part of our baseball program for the past three springs. The players and coaches have benefited from Big Mike as much as he has benefited from being involved with our program."

Over the course of the years, Big Mike has been a part of many conference, district, and regional championships and one state championship. In no other time in the history of Hudsonville High School have our baseball and basketball programs seen this much collective success. I would like to call this the "Big Mike factor."

Regardless of the room he is in or the playing field he is on, Big Mike has the ability to set the climate by showing his constantly positive attitude, smile, and laugh. His selflessness, along with his undying love for his teammates, rubs off on each member of the team. All he wants is for the team to succeed. Having the opportunity to present Big Mike with his very own varsity jacket will not only go down as one of my favorite moments of 2014 but one of my favorite moments in my professional life. Listening to the applause and seeing tears stream down the faces of peers and adults only validated the impact he has had on this school and community.

As we start a new year, how about we all take the "Big Mike Challenge" and work to *set* the climate around us instead of reflecting it. Why is setting the climate so hard for us to do?

In order to set the climate, we must take a risk, and whenever risk is involved, people are afraid to fail. The Big Mike Challenge, however, is foolproof. We simply cannot fail if we live life putting others before ourselves and maintaining a positive attitude in every situation. The next time we're forced to either endure a bad game or deal with some other type of adversity, we need to recall the Big Mike Challenge. As a parent, the next time you feel the need to talk negatively about another player or coach, take the Big Mike Challenge. Or if a decision was made that may not seem to be in the best interest of your child, again, take the Big Mike Challenge. My hope is that if we can all live our lives a little more like Michael Kempema, we can create a more positive culture within our own communities.

Fast Forward: "Big Mike" just finished his eighth year as the manager for our basketball and baseball teams. He continues to be a staple in our athletic program, positively impacting student athletes and coaches every day. The "Big Mike factor" is real and we are thankful to have him here at Hudsonville to help cultivate our culture.

Inside the Huddle

What is your greatest "sports memory" moment involving one of your children? What made it so special?

Executing the Play

Regardless of your child's playing time on the team, write a letter to the coach expressing thanks for the time and commitment he or she dedicates to the program.

30 Second Timeout

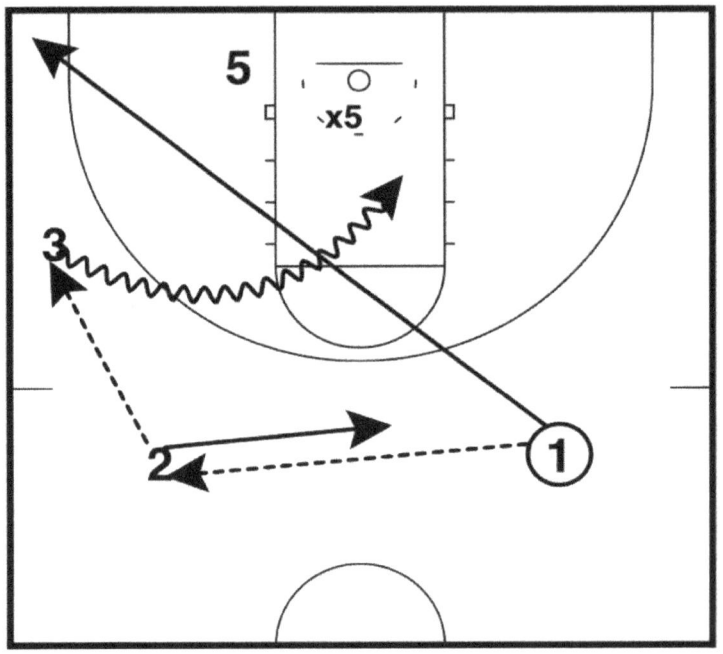

WHAT IS YOUR IMAGE?

Football Toss, Plinko, Tic-Tac-Toe, and Balloon Pop are all popular games we have played at carnivals. When I was a kid, my favorite carnival activity was the room full of mirrors. My friends and I would laugh as our bodies were distorted in different ways depending on the mirror we stood in front of. I loved the mirror that made me look tall. As a basketball player, I always felt that a few extra inches would give me an advantage over my opponent.

Carnival mirrors can also be a metaphor for our lives. We sometimes look to distort our own image as a means of looking better than or gaining an "advantage" over our neighbors, friends, teammates, and co-workers. The avenues through which we most often distort our image are social media outlets like Facebook, Twitter, Snapchat, and Instagram.

There we see people post their child's accomplishments for the whole world to see. Some perceive this as posturing: positioning ourselves in front of others and yelling, "Hey, look at us--we have it all figured out! Our children are special and our lives are great!" The fact is, however, most people are dealing with the same issues and insecurities as everyone else.

Because I also feel that burst of pride when my own kids perform well, I completely understand why we do this as parents. However, it is dangerous to use social media as a platform to showcase our children's accomplishments.

One danger is rooted in the idea that our children's performance is central to their value as people, hence creating a distorted image. That is why it is important to say, "I love to watch you play" instead of "You played great tonight." What happens when they do not perform well? What do we say then? What are we saying to our children when we *don't* post about them because they performed poorly? Do our actions indicate that we equate our children's value with their performance?

Social Media Challenge.

Analyze your last five social media posts and ask the following questions:

- Why did I post this?
- Did this post distort your image to make yourself look better?
- Is this post a true reflection of yourself?

In a leadership class at Hudsonville, we presented this challenge to students so they could gain a new perspective on their posts and the image they had actually attempted to portray. The teacher used his social media posts as an example and asked the class what they had learned about him from his posts. A student remarked that the teacher was trying to be funny. Upon hearing this, the teacher cringed because, as a middle child, his way of getting attention from his parents was to make jokes. Humor was his distorted image.

One of the greatest attributes we can ever teach our children is humility. Humility when we achieve success and humility as we battle through adversity. Humility has no mirrors because it is one image that can never be distorted. Humility is genuine and sincere.

The next time you talk about your child with a co-worker or post something on social media, pause and ask yourself, "Is this a true image of our family or is it closer to the reflection in a carnival mirror?"

Inside the Huddle
When parents just focus on the performance of their own children, does it have an impact on the culture of the team? Why or why not?

Executing the Play
Make sure all of your social media posts center around team accomplishments and/or include as many individual members of the team as possible.

30 Second Timeout

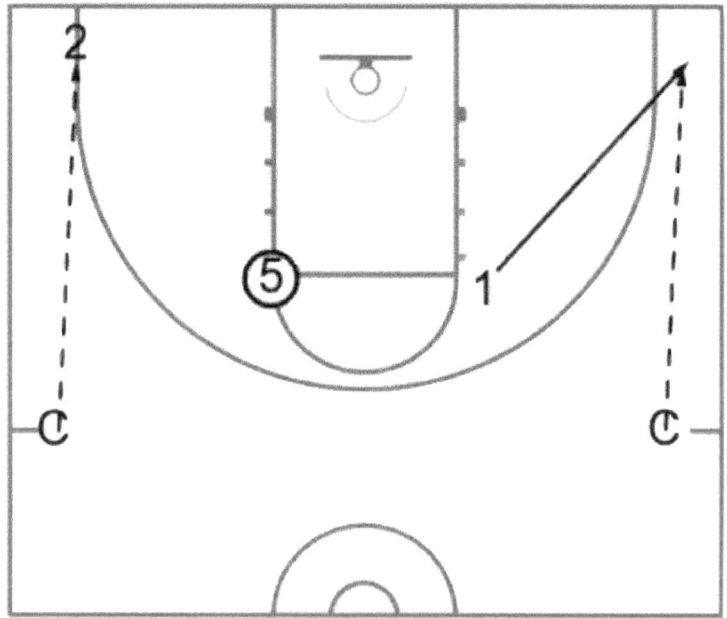

YOU SEE WHAT YOU WANT TO SEE

Number 81.

Every fall Saturday afternoon since 2017, I've watched number 81 play for the Arizona Wildcats. Occasionally during a game, he is on the line of scrimmage and I can't see his number, but I am still able to locate him because he has a white towel hanging from the back of his pants. I love watching my nephew Bryce compete, and I find that on every single play I focus solely on him. Sometimes I will watch him block and I don't even notice who has the ball. When he runs a passing route, I instinctively believe he is the only one open. I watch the entire game with tunnel vision, focusing only on one player: Number 81.

How often do we do that with our own kids? For every second of every game, we watch every move they make. As parents, we should consider a couple of interesting perspectives when we do this. For example, when I merely watch my own child, I might focus on every good thing he or she does, whether or not it has any impact on the game. However, when my son or daughter is on the bench, I watch the game differently. Now my attention shifts to the other players, and I might find myself watching for any mistakes they make in order to validate why my kid should be playing. I will see what I want to see. This is called tunnel vision, and tunnel vision can be a dangerous way to watch our children compete because it becomes all about them and less about the team.

This has become the million-dollar question in high school athletics: Do I want my son or daughter to play all the time on a poor team or be a role player on a championship team? I often have these conversations with student-athletes who struggle with the perception that when they are not "seen," they are not considered a valued member of the team. In reality, they are "seen" by their coaches and teammates every day in practice, playing crucial roles in helping their team become the best it can be. My hope is that the memories they create with their teammates while winning championships far outweigh seeing their names in newspaper clippings.

As an athletic director over the last eight years, I have had the opportunity to watch thousands of games from a different perspective. I love watching the dig that leads to a set and then a kill. I love the hustle play in basketball that sparks a fast break. I love the extra pass in a soccer game that results in a goal. I love watching the ball move from side to side in water polo, ending with a pass in the hole and an eventual goal. I love watching the kids on the deck during a swim meet cheer on the last leg of a relay. I love watching a player bunt to score a runner on third. I love to watch a defensive end in football force a quarterback to move up into the pocket where the linebacker meets him for a sack. I love to watch a wrestler come from behind in the closing seconds of a match, his teammates stomping in support on the wood bleachers. I love to watch a lacrosse player fight for a ground ball and pass it to a teammate on the other end of the field who then scores a goal. I love to watch a doubles player hit an incredible return that leads to an overhead winner by her partner. I love to watch a hurdler in track and then be amazed by the 3200-meter distance runner. I love to watch a bowler roll a strike and have both teams congratulate him on the way off the lane. I love to watch the cheer team execute a stunt because of the incredible synergy it requires. I love to watch every skater on the ice touch the puck that finds the back of the net. I love watching the long ball in golf, along with the up and down sand save...

Yes, I love watching my nephew play football, but lately, I have also grown an appreciation for how much his team has improved from the beginning of the year to the end. That improvement is not based on one player alone, but rather a collection of young men committed to getting better each and every day for the success of their team. Sports are beautiful to watch when we eliminate tunnel vision. The next time you are at a game, I challenge each of you to watch the *whole* game. Your experience will be greater and your anxiety as a parent will decline. Let's all see as much as we can possibly see.

Inside the Huddle
What percentage of time do you devote to just watching the performance of your son or daughter as opposed to the whole team? What are some benefits to watching and supporting everyone?

Executing the Play
After your child's next game, seek out a player on the team who did something noteworthy, whether it was cheering on the team from the bench, showing sportsmanship, or performing well. Do this verbally or through a text to the family or individual.

30 Second Timeout

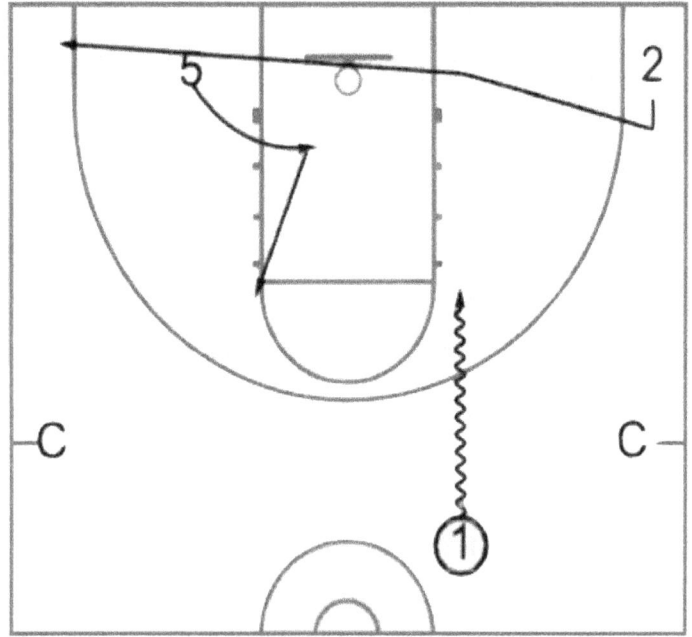

IMPACT OF BODY LANGUAGE IN SPORTS

Have you ever gone to a game and, the entire time, watched the players on the bench? The answer for most of us is likely "no" because the reason we go to games is to watch the action of the competition take place. However, watching the bench can tell you a great deal about the players on the team and the culture that has been created. The next time you are at a game, take notice of the player who was just taken out, as well as the players who are on the bench for most or all of the game. What does their body language express to their teammates, coaches, opponents, and the spectators?

Recently, I went to a college football game in which the starting quarterback was taken out after the second series. The starter had hardly come off the field over the last two and a half seasons, so he was naturally surprised by this unannounced decision. But instead of being outwardly upset and isolating himself from his team, he made it a point to verbally encourage each of the offensive linemen. He had no time to feel sorry for himself; his role had changed on the team and his teammates were watching their leader to see how he would respond. Two series later he reentered the contest and, on the second play from scrimmage, ran for a 60-yard touchdown. On the next series, he threw a touchdown pass. The offensive linemen blocked harder than ever to protect their quarterback, the one who encouraged them while he faced adversity.

Body language can have such a positive and direct impact on a game.

How often have you seen a player, on his way to the bench, untuck his jersey and go sit by himself without acknowledging anyone else? What prompted his reaction was the coach's decision to take him out of the game. This body language can upset the rest of the team because it sends the message that he values his own playing time over the team's performance. This selfish behavior is disappointing to the players who regularly sit on the bench because they would love the opportunity to participate. Instead, they are left to cheer for a teammate whose greatest concern is himself. The other team will then thrive off of that selfish body language because negative reactions demonstrate weakness, and the appearance of weakness provides opponents more confidence.

As I recently watched a closely contested freshman girls basketball game, I noticed an opposing team's player sitting back in her chair, upset at her lack of playing time. The coach turned around to tell the player to check-in but stopped at the sight of the disgruntled look on her face. She immediately told her that for as long as she kept that attitude, she would continue to sit. Her body language revealed her emotions. Later in the fourth quarter, that same girl who had been sitting back in her chair was now cheering for her teammates. The coach noticed and checked her into the game. That coach held her accountable and taught her player a valuable life lesson about body language and attitude.

How often, as a parent, have you commented on the bench performance of your children? Have you ever acknowledged the positive attitude or enthusiasm they displayed on the bench as they cheered on their teammates? Have you held them accountable for their negative body language on the bench or on the floor? As a parent, you may find yourself not knowing what to say after a contest in which your kids did not play. Simply watching how they interact with their teammates can help facilitate a conversation.

Recognizing your child's positive attitude on the bench will help him or her feel valued in a society that can seem to focus only on performance. The next time you go to a game, watch those athletes on the bench and how they react to their teammates as well as how the players on the floor react as they're being taken out. Body language can have a significant impact on the culture of any team, and we must make this a priority as youth sports continue to impact the growth of our kids.

Inside the Huddle
In what ways does body language set up a team for success or failure? Provide some examples of when you have witnessed both.

Executing the Play
The next time you watch a game, pay attention to your child's body language while on the bench, both during the game and at the conclusion of the contest. Report back to him or her with a "bench camera" grade.

30 Second Timeout

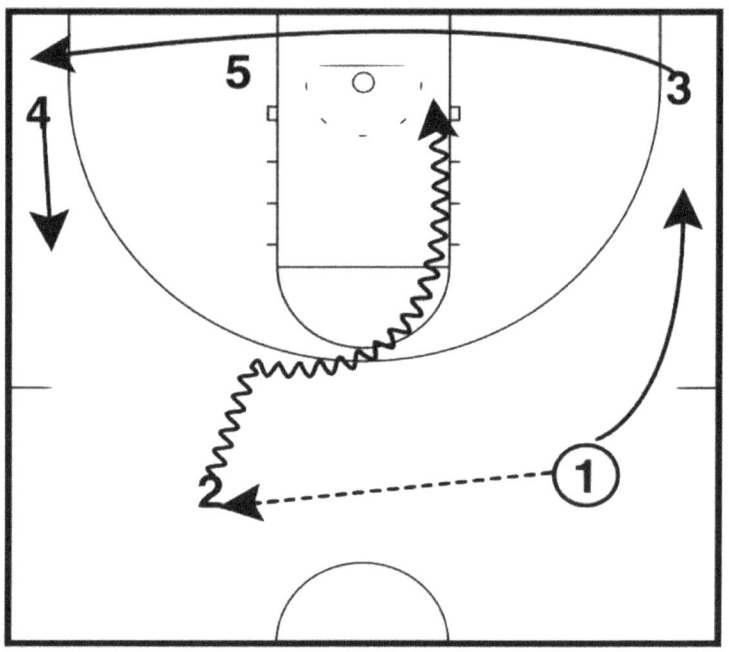

IT'S OVER

A simple service return that landed into the net ended my son's tennis career. Part of being a senior means having to face end dates, and just like that, he was done. It seems like yesterday I was playing catch with him in the front yard. It seems like yesterday I was rebounding as he shot at our basketball hoop. And, it seems like yesterday I put a tennis racquet in his hands for the first time. All the success and failure, along with the laughter and frustration, simply ended.

Along the way people would warn me about how fast the time goes, but living day to day, I didn't really believe them. Going into the final match of the season, it occurred to me that this would be the last day I would watch my son play competitive tennis, but it didn't really hit me until I watched that last ball go into the net. At the same time, I also realized that we would be experiencing many final moments during his senior year and that this was a natural part of the journey. What I didn't know on that day was that this would actually be the very last time I would see him compete. The cancellation of spring sports due to the COVID-19 crisis took from him the opportunity to participate in what would have been his final season of track and field.

We never know when things will be taken away from us.

Because of the shutdown, my daughter, also a senior, will not have the opportunity to finish her tennis career at Hudsonville. For the two of us, tennis is more than a sport. It is our connection. Since she was five years old hitting foam balls in the gym, the tennis court has been far more than a surface with lines and a net. It has been our place of solitude. We've hit thousands and thousands of tennis balls over the years, but more importantly, the tennis court created a platform where lessons were shared, stories of success and failure were told, and a love for a sport was born. I've dreaded the day the tennis court sits silent, because that means my daughter will be moving on to her next stage in life. That time is now.

Sports are not the end-all, and they surely do not define a person. However, they can work as a mechanism to bring people together. They can teach life lessons that are often taken for granted--until something abruptly ends and we're sharply reminded of their importance.

The purpose of this article is not to talk about the end as much as it is to emphasize the importance of those moments leading *to* the end. Don't let those moments slip away. If your son or daughter asks you to go outside and play catch, please put down the computer or phone and do it. The email can wait. The phone call can wait. The game on TV can wait. Admittedly, I have been occasionally guilty of this as well, but I now realize the importance of time and how unpredictable it can be. I have one more chance with my youngest daughter to make sure we don't take those moments for granted. They are moments we will never get back, and again, we never know when these moments could run out.

As a high school athletic director, all I've wanted was more time. Sixty plus-hour work weeks while trying to navigate work and home schedules are often extremely challenging. Many of us live this life every day. We all would like more time.

Ironically, since one 48-hour span during the month of March 2020, it seems like all I've had is time. In those two days, after Rudy Gorbet tested positive for COVID-19, both the NCAA and NBA shut down while schools and businesses began closing their doors indefinitely. Now, time is all many of us have. My hope is that we all appreciate time as a gift that must be accepted when given. We need to take advantage of this time and regain a perspective on what is really important in our lives and then act on that. These moments, too, will eventually run out, and our lives will resume as many of us again attempt to juggle personal, work, and sports schedules. Are we ready? During this "time off" from the busyness of life, are we focusing on how we can maximize every moment of every day?

For some of us, this gives us a chance to hit the restart button and maybe look at youth sports through a different lens. Maybe our interactions with our kids, coaches, and officials will be more positive. Maybe we will worry less about an outcome and more about the process. Once we get back to the playing field, maybe we will look at participation in sports differently. Just maybe, more of us will understand that it is truly a gift, and every gift deserves a level of gratitude toward the many people who allow the experience, and all its life lessons, to transpire.

Years from now, when we look back at the year of COVID-19, will we still value the essence of time and living in the moment? Will we still sincerely appreciate the gift of sports? Each one of us wants to look back at our kids' experiences with athletics and have no regrets. No regrets with our actions. No regrets with our time. We have an opportunity as parents right now to pause, reflect, and make changes that could impact youth sports for generations to come. We must seize the opportunity now because this part of life will be over before we know it. For some of us, maybe even more quickly than we expect.

Inside the Huddle
What is the purpose of this sports journey you have gone on with your kids? What do you want them to get out of this experience?

Executing the Play
Watch every sports event your kids play in like it might be their last.

About the Author

Kevin Wolma currently serves as the athletic director at Hudsonville High School where he also teaches leadership classes. During his tenure in the district he has also taught physical education and health while coaching over 30 seasons of tennis, basketball, and golf. Kevin would love for you to connect with him at kwolma22@gmail.com or through Twitter @KevinWolma.

Visit the *30 Second Timeout Website* at:

30secondtimeout.weebly/com

CPSIA information can be obtained
at www.ICGtesting.com
Printed in the USA
LVHW092045240620
658899LV00012B/1649